D1523023

Hey, That Could Be a Business!

PETER RICCHIUTI
Annette Naake Sisco

Out to Lunch is a production of INO Broadcasting, Inc.

Our cover was designed by Tim Banfell

This book is a revised version of "Being Your Own Boss Is Terrific"
by Peter Ricchiuti published in 2021.

ISBN: 979-8-35093-186-0

Also by Peter Ricchiuti

Stocks Under Rocks: How to Uncover Overlooked, Profitable Market Opportunities

By Peter Ricchiuti and Anthony Wood

Equity Research

Peter dedicates this book to his wife, Laurie, and his sons, Matthew and William. Really, who else but my immediate family would put up with me?

From Annette, to my family.

CONTENTS

FOREWORD

By Rob Lalka

Too often, we celebrate entrepreneurs as heroes who "have what it takes," and then spend all our time debating what "it" is: gumption, grit, stick-to-it-iveness...or whatever expression we can come up with to capture that iconoclast-against-the-world ideal.

The reality is, as always, much different from the stories we tell ourselves. I have found that success in entrepreneurial ventures often depends on an individual's willingness to go far beyond their own experience. As I tell my students, if you're building for yourself, you'll have one customer. If you're building for others, you can capture a market by solving their problems in new and unique ways. The adage I repeat to reinforce this principle is: "*Your* world is not *the* world."

In other words, understanding customers takes humility, and it also takes empathy. It means questioning your own assumptions and challenging yourself to see things from other points of view. It's all about learning from others, listening deeply, finding opportunities where others haven't, and building something great that you probably never would've imagined when you first set out to solve a problem.

Entrepreneurs create the next generation of businesses, so they inevitably need to be "skating to where the puck is going, not where it's been," to paraphrase Wayne Gretzky. What are we learning that the next generation wants, even demands?

Here are a couple of surprising insights. According to the Deloitte Global Millennial survey, "Millennials say that making a positive difference in the world is more important to them than professional recognition" and "millennials rank creating social value as the primary purpose of business — not creating profit."

As you wrap your mind around that, listen closely. You might hear a distant, shuffling sound — that's Milton Friedman rolling over in his grave. But here's the thing. Entrepreneurs who understand this from the outset — those who see climate risk as business risk, who believe diversity and inclusivity are as important to their HR as to their PR — they'll build better businesses in both senses of the word.

That's what the market is telling us about what's to come. The future of business is not just about maximizing profit for the shareholder, but also about answering a wider array of concerns from many stakeholders, including employees, customers, the communities where they live, and even the planet for future generations.

Don't take it from me, though. BlackRock CEO Larry Fink has more money under management than anybody since Alexander the Great (over $9 trillion as of this writing, in midsummer 2021). Here's his take: "Without a sense of purpose, no company, either public or private, can achieve its full potential. It will ultimately lose the license to operate from key stakeholders." In fact, he's called this a "fundamental reshaping of finance" and argued that "ultimately, *purpose* is the engine of long-term profitability."

The entrepreneurs who will achieve greatness within this new paradigm won't be the ones who imagine themselves as Future Great Men of History steamrolling towards their preordained destinies.

They'll be the ones who have confidence about their purpose, yet the empathy to understand other points of view; they'll have the humility to take time to listen when they're wrong and be determined to always improve with each new day.

And they'll be the committed, passionate, resilient and caring people who end up building great businesses that employees, customers and communities truly love.

Rob Lalka

Albert R. Lepage Professor in Business

Executive Director, Albert Lepage Center for Entrepreneurship and Innovation

A.B. Freeman School of Business, Tulane University

New Orleans

INTRODUCTION

You may be surprised to find yourself reading a book about business. Perhaps you thought such a publication would be torturous, boring and reserved for the bed-ridden and imprisoned. Or maybe you're just out of Ambien.

But I love this stuff. When it comes to business, I'm usually the most interested guy in the room. I'm forever curious about how people and companies make their money.

Fortunately, I have a venue to both entertain people and share this thing for work, commerce and innovation. For the last decade I have hosted a weekly business show called "Out to Lunch." The show airs on WWNO, National Public Radio in New Orleans and is also available as a podcast.

Each Tuesday, I invite two entrepreneurs to lunch. Most of these lunches have taken place at Commander's Palace, arguably one of the finest restaurants in America. Others take place at a terrific beer and pizza joint called NOLA Brewing. It's famous for replicating NYC water to make its New York style pizza. Hey, it tastes great.

I'm never sure if these guests actually want to be on the show or are lured in by the free food and drink. (Free lunch! Take that, economists!)

It's interesting to be on the radio because people never know what you look like. I met a guy who said, "Oh, you're the host of that lunch show. I thought you would be fatter." Gee, how do you respond to that?

It's a friendly, personality-driven show where we discuss the trials and joys of running your own business. I simply can't hold in these stories any longer. I've hosted 400 lunches and I've included some of the most interesting ones in this book.

You'll notice that these businesses aren't high-flying, complex ventures out of Silicon Valley. One guest explained to me the many ins and outs of his business and then added, "But, hey, it's not exactly the Manhattan Project." They're generally un-sexy but inspiring examples of successful inspiration and innovation.

After listening to our shows, listeners often tell me, "I could have come up with that!" But, here's the thing: They didn't, and these people did.

Think of this as entrepreneurship for the rest of us. Each and every one of these people worked very hard to make their business succeed.

Lauren Siegel is the director of brand and culture at Trepwise (trepwise. com), a growth consulting firm. She believes that starting and running a business is truly the American dream. She has helped lots and lots of those dreams come true. It's wonderful, but, "There's an element of loneliness in starting and running a business," she says. These people most often need technical help and support. Like Lauren's clients, the majority of my guests came into the world of entrepreneurship with no formal business education. ("What are these parentheses in our accounts?")

These folks "could really benefit from the advice, wisdom and camaraderie of a small circle of fellow entrepreneurs who have traveled the same road," Lauren says.

She says that being an entrepreneur can be lonely. Sometimes you need to remind yourself that when you're alone, you're in good company.

Some guests have talked about entrepreneurs having a different set of issues and problems from salaried (even highly paid) business leaders. One told me that at most functions he doesn't feel like he fits in.

There are a great many reasons to go into business for yourself. This book is put together to look at dozens of them.

Most observers see the money going into the cash register, but don't recognize all the money spent to keep that business going. We can't forget that the money "going out" includes taxes. (I explained taxes to my children by eating 38% of their ice cream.)

And, at least in the first few years, starting a business is more work, more difficult and more time-consuming than whatever you're currently doing.

Unlike the makeup of traditional corporate America, the majority of our guests on "Out to Lunch" are women and minorities, and they come from a wide array of places and backgrounds.

Not all of these ventures are meant to generate big profits. Starting a non-profit presents similar challenges. These entrepreneurs often see opportunities in communities that others overlook, and their impact and success is measured in more than dollars and cents.

You probably know that many entrepreneurial ventures fail. What might surprise you is that generally, intrepid business owners don't look at such setbacks as defeats. Each of these washouts taught them valuable lessons. They wear their setbacks as badges of honor and can't wait, both on and off air, to tell me about them. One guest gave me a particularly honest assessment when he said, "Peter, I've started several businesses and they don't all work out. You win some, you lose some. And some get rained out."

In fact, nearly all of my guests have tried and "failed" at starting other businesses, and each of them has ideas for still more new businesses just up their sleeves. They're often referred to as serial entrepreneurs and simply can't imagine working for anyone else ever again.

Many of the guests start their businesses as a side hustle. This allows them to develop (and get the kinks out) of their ventures while maintaining a steady paycheck. Choosing to operate only their businesses is a difficult and decisive moment for an entrepreneur.

Millions of Baby Boomers retire each year. Some of the most well-prepared entrepreneurs started their enterprise as a kind of second act. These are people who completed successful careers at an established firm and want to fulfill a dream of starting something from the ground up.

These new adventures begin as both profit and non-profit organizations. Many tell the story of retiring and learning that their significant other wasn't really interested in having them around all the time. There's an old expression for this: "I married you for better or worse, but I didn't marry you for lunch." Sweet but direct.

My guests have redefined, and customized, the "American Dream" of running your own enterprise. The folks in this book seek to enjoy financial success. But, as we say in Louisiana, there's also lagniappe (a Creole term meaning a little something extra). It's difficult to measure the benefits of being your own boss and "running the show."

My hope is that the next pages inspire you to chase your dreams — and have fun doing it.

CHAPTER 1.

Pursue Your Passion

Laken Swan, Lauren Bercier: Something Borrowed Blooms
Bella Blue: New Orleans School of Burlesque

Passion is to entrepreneurs what spinach is to Popeye. If there's one ingredient that is essential for the success of a new business idea, it's passion. Founding your dream business is seldom easy, but a passion for your idea keeps the energy flowing.

Passion is also that special love that fuels human relationships. A couple of my favorite entrepreneurs found the intersection of those kinds of passion when they created Something Borrowed Blooms, ultra-luxe silk flowers that brides show off for their special day, then return — an environmentally friendly and affordable way to celebrate their wedding. It's the intersection of a passion for sustainability and love.

For burlesque dancer Bella Blue, the art form of dance is her passion — and sparks passion in her admiring audience.

What's YOUR passion?

Something Borrowed Blooms

Laken Swan was in that season of her life. She felt like she was going to a wedding every weekend. Many were lavish celebrations with hundreds of guests, carefully coordinated outfits and sumptuous feasts. Amid the meticulously planned celebrations, Laken couldn't help but wonder about the sacrifices young couples were making for their special day. And, being a member of the environmentally conscious millennial generation, she also wondered what happened to those cut flowers and other decorations the day after the wedding.

At that stage of life, just the cost of attending these back-to-back-to-back events leaves you pretty broke. (This in spite of the youthful mantra: I can't be out of money, I still have checks left!)

As a marketing executive with a sense of style, Laken often borrowed designer clothes and accessories from the online supplier Rent the Runway. Founded in 2009 by two women who met at Harvard Business School, Rent the Runway lets customers wear "statement" clothing for a fraction of the cost of buying it — then return it for someone else to wear.

Many products are now part of this sharing economy, like Uber, Airbnb and co-working spaces. Looking for a business idea, Laken and her cousin, Lauren Bercier, thought of the costly, luxurious wedding flowers that are used one day, then discarded. It might sound crazy, but it wasn't all that long ago that renting a car online was a novel idea too. Could flowers be saved and shared?

Turns out, the answer is yes. Ultra-high-quality silk blooms are so perfect that they are virtually indistinguishable from the real thing. To own, they are pricey. But to borrow for a day? Not so much.

So, in 2015, Laken and Lauren founded "Something Borrowed Blooms," a company that, four years later, was shipping arrangements of peonies, roses, baby's breath and more to as many as 450 weddings a month.

"We hand-select every single stem," Laken says. "We'll dedicate days to just sourcing and curating one collection. Lots of thought and detail go into picking out each individual stem and the greenery included in each collection."

These flowers are a far cry from those awful, faded, dusty plastic flowers sitting in a bouquet above your grandmother's television. This is not that at all. These flowers look great, and they smell great.

"Our boxes are actually scented, so when the blooms arrive to the bride and she opens up the box, the flowers have that smell and create those memories that you get with fresh flowers," Laken tells me.

Laken is SBB's chief marketing officer, a trade she learned working for Caesars Entertainment. Say what you will about casinos, those guys know more about their customers than any industry on the planet. While Laken started the flower rental business as a way to use her creative talents, she finds herself leaning hard on the skills she learned in marketing analytics — a very data-driven field.

Laken has devoted herself to learning about her clients — young couples who want luxury without breaking the bank. A typical order of cut wedding flowers, costing $2,500 or $3,000, could be replaced by silk rentals for about $500. The couple might want to put those savings toward a special honeymoon — or maybe a pair of JetSkis!

Equally important, these millennials like the idea of flowers that aren't thrown out after the wedding.

"They're using it for 30 minutes to an hour for their ceremony, but they are able to pass it on to someone else," Laken says.

Right now, SBB delivers those fresh-scented wedding flowers everywhere in the U.S. and Canada (except Hawaii). FedEx

loves these people! A few months after Laken was on the show I began seeing banners in FedEx stores showing Laken, Lauren and their business. Now, that's making it.

A giant warehouse in Lafayette, Louisiana, stores the company's collections, which are continuously expanded and refreshed.

"Sometime in the future we'll definitely have to look at multiple distribution points," Laken says.

Do people steal the stuff? Laken says not, but maybe she hangs out with a better class of people than some of us.

"Every now and then a groom's boutonniere will go missing, but it's not a big deal," she says.

The New Orleans School of Burlesque

Bella Blue began training as a ballet dancer at age 3 and studied ballet and modern dance until adulthood. But in 2007, she stepped out in a sultry spotlight, joining the historic ranks of burlesque dancers. It's an art form she fell in love with and has helped to preserve and promote ever since, through performances in New Orleans' famed nightclubs. And it's a business that she launched as the founder and headmistress of the New Orleans School of Burlesque.

Her students are all ages and they are there for many different reasons, from bucket lists to birthdays.

"Sometimes it's 'I'm getting married.' Sometimes it's 'I'm getting divorced.' Sometimes it's 'I just wanted to see, I'm just curious.' You name it, that person has come through the room," she says.

Whatever their motivation, students learn the confidence-building, sexy appeal of "the art of striptease," she says.

Bella's business is solidly grounded in the work ethic of classical ballet.

"Ballet is a huge part, and it gives you structure," she says. Producing as many as 26 shows a month, plus teaching, running the school and serving as a spokesperson for the local burlesque revival, the perseverance she gained through ballet came in handy.

Burlesque is a storytelling dance form, in which elaborate costumes, seductive moves and showmanship lead the audience on a fantasy journey. The nostalgic appeal has had a renaissance in recent years.

The dance became popular in New Orleans in the mid-1880s, Bella says. In its heyday, between the 1930s and the 1960s, you could see up to 50 burlesque acts a night on Bourbon Street. It went underground for a while, banned by authorities and later outgunned by less subtle shows at strip clubs.

But apparently, there's a market for subtlety. In the 1980s, burlesque came back.

"New Orleans and New York are kind of the two hubs for burlesque — and looking at the burlesque revival, it's kind of happening again," Bella says.

I asked Bella about the difference between stripping and burlesque.

"About $900 a night," she quips, referring to the very generous tips earned by "exotic dancers" at strip clubs.

But all jesting aside, she defends both dance forms.

"To insult one is to insult the other," the ebullient dancer says earnestly, "because club stripping came out of burlesque. To each his own."

The real difference between the two, she says, is that the strip club acts are "super tactile, in your face, and there's not too much of a tease element. You can pretty much see what you want to see.

"In burlesque, you have your act, you have to take them through your storyline. At the end, the audience is less enthralled with the fact you are nearly naked and more excited about how you got there."

The school offers walk-in classes and private lessons. Bella stays busy producing and performing in shows, wowing audiences with her fabulous dance moves, costumes and makeup.

I once attended a burlesque show. I brought my old college roommate with me, and we both loved it. The place was so packed that the preferred seats on the floor had already been filled and we were banished to the balcony. The entertainment started with a comedian and was followed by a jazz band. When the star of the show got into the finer parts of her act, an older gentleman actually fainted. When the felled patron and his friend were escorted out, my friend asked me if we could run down and grab their seats. That seemed low, even for us.

Patrons' behavior notwithstanding, Bella loves being the face of burlesque.

"I always have glitter on," she says. Glitter? The so-called herpes of theater, that turns up in every crevice of every room?

"You can't get rid of it," Bella acknowledges. "And why would you want to?"

Peter's Principles #1

Standup comic Rodney Dangerfield joked that as a kid, he had a lemonade stand that made no money—so he had to burn it down for the insurance money. Let's not use Rodney as our guide to business ethics!

It's your business. Be prepared to work harder than you ever have when working for someone else. Not a soul has the same dedication to the business as the owner. Nobody has ever washed a rented car.

CHAPTER 2.

You'll Have a Story to Tell

Betsy Bellard: Zydeco Chop Chop
Tara Guidry: Cajun Crate

Troy Primeaux: Primo Peppers
Phil Gremillion: Papa Jeabert's "penis" peppers

The food culture of South Louisiana is justly famous around the world. Abundant seafood, long growing seasons and rich cultural diversity have come together to create this delicious way of life.

The Lafayette area has strong ties to its French roots and the language is sometimes heard there. However, a couple of generations ago families striving for assimilation into American life discouraged their children from speaking French. Sadly, French is heard less and less.

I once saw a bumper sticker that read "Poor Louisiana! So far from France, so close to Texas."

Cajun culture is carefully tended in home kitchens across Acadiana, where opinions on the best sausage or jambalaya recipe can vary fiercely from town to town. It's a culture that has nurtured many businesses over the years, from tiny restaurants to the international giant Tabasco.

Small businesses based on food can be some of the most successful, and satisfying, around. Whether it's Grandma's recipe or a carefully cultivated backyard pepper, these small-business people are sharing something they love deeply with the world.

Zydeco Chop Chop, Cajun Crate

People in Acadiana take their cooking seriously. Many dishes start in a cast-iron skillet, with a combination of chopped herbs and vegetables familiar to every Cajun as the "holy trinity": onion, celery, bell pepper. Later, add garlic, parsley and more. In 2008, Tim Bellard came up with a dehydrated blend of those ingredients that gives cooks quick and easy access to Cajun flavor. Headquartered in the Opelousas area, Zydeco Chop Chop is sold in grocery stores across South Louisiana – and that's how you know it's the real deal. Third-generation owner Betsy Bellard is carrying on the family tradition, which began with meat and poultry businesses in Opelousas. The aromatic mix is shipped all over the country.

Cajun flavors have fans everywhere. That was the impetus for another Acadiana food business: Cajun Crate, what I like to call the Amazon.com of Cajun food products, and the brainchild of Lafayette's Tara Guidry.

"What got me into Cajun Crate is that most of my family lives out of state, and so they are all on Amazon trying to buy stuff," Tara says. Spices, jambalaya mix, the kind of beans your mama made – the taste of South Louisiana is not on the shelf in your typical suburban American supermarket.

"This is a problem we all have," Tara says, referring to the food-loving denizens of Acadiana. "If you are from this area and you have someone who lives out of state, you are always sending some type of care packages. 'Here's your roux, here's your coffee, here's your hot sauce.'"

After Tara left her job as operations manager of a computer store chain in order to care for her first baby, she wanted to start her own business. Her husband had already come up with an idea.

"He said, 'You should start a subscription box and call it Cajun Crate.' I got online and got the dot com domain and said, 'Let's do it.'"

The idea resonated with the busy young mom, who subscribed to a diaper service, among other necessities. Cajun Crate sends out monthly boxes to hungry Cajun expats. Gift boxes are also popular. The website is a lively center of information with "Cajun bait" recipes that just couldn't be more authentic ("Cajun Bait Alligator Sauce Piquante: Cut alligator jaw meat in bite-size pieces...")

Tara also ships plenty of products close to home. When the coronavirus pandemic made shopping trips dicey, her orders boomed. With products like Zydeco Chop Chop and Swampadelic Hot Sauce plus Cajun Crate's delivery, you could be anywhere and still make gumbo.

I once interviewed the CEO of a very large hot sauce company who suggested many uses for their product. This included putting a drop into your morning coffee. I shared this novel idea with my wife, who immediately pointed out, "Peter, the man sells hot sauce!" She definitely had a point.

Tara says she loves being her own boss and has spun off a couple of other ventures. She enjoys helping other businesses in her community grow by giving them a nationwide platform to market their goods. When we spoke, she was at work creating a food hub and incubator in Lafayette to allow smaller businesses to prepare food, store it and ship it.

Primo's Peppers, Papa Jeabert's

Troy "Primo" Primeaux runs his Primo's Peppers like an artist runs a studio. In the world of pepper growers, Primo is a celebrity. He farms his award-winning peppers, bottles the sauce like craft beer, and is hands-on everywhere from the garden to delivery. A former rock musician, Primo also studied nursing, but finally chose horticulture. Today, he markets The Farmer's Daughter hot pepper jellies, plus sauces that range from "hot" to "Swampadelic" ("Hotter'n the Devil's Pecker!"). C'mon, admit it. These names are pretty catchy!

Pepper growers in Louisiana take a lot of pride in their products. Primo's website lists a host of prizes for taste and marketing. But a major standard for pepper products is, of course, heat. That jalapeno on your sandwich rates a pleasantly invigorating 2,500-8,000 Scoville Heat Units. Tabasco peppers kick in at 30,000-50,000, and habaneros will really wake you up at 350,000 Scovilles. It's getting hot in here!

But those numbers pale in comparison to the red-hot 7-Pot Primo Pepper, a barn burner at almost 1.3 million Scovilles. That's the fiery little pepper Primo developed himself and uses in his "monster" Primo's Peppers Swampadelic Sauce.

Who buys this stuff? You might be surprised to learn sales of Primeaux's most potent pepper sauce are highest not in Acadiana, but out of state. Ohio and Pennsylvania have amazing numbers of "chiliheads," Primo says. Maybe they're looking for an antidote to all that snow and ice!

Primo's business is small and hand-crafted, and that's the way he likes it. With a wife and young child, he's got plenty to keep him busy. Although the margins on blast-furnace-hot pepper sauce are not high—a bottle might last two years. Still, business is good. "It's way profitable," he says. "More profitable than I would have imagined."

Another pepper guru we spoke to in 2017: Phil Gremillion, of Papa Jeabert's out of Lafayette. His claim to fame is a rare pepper which, aside from being so hot it has to be processed in a hazmat suit and gas mask, bears the unique distinction of looking like an undersized penis. These "peter peppers" can be easily grown at home, if you can source a few seeds and don't mind playing host to the winner of Organic Garden Magazine's "Most Pornographic Pepper" award.

I've recently planted a few of these seeds myself. Ideally, I would like to propagate this variety and serve as a kind of Johnny Appleseed for these conversation starters. "Mom, how did these things get here? Well, son, there was this Tulane professor ..."

Everybody's gotta eat. If you have a recipe, a home-grown product or a kitchen gadget idea that your family loves, it could be the next small business sensation!

Peter's Principles #2

Overnight success is incredibly rare. Several guests on my radio show have said that things began to turn around just before they were about to "fold up the tent, pick up stakes, turn in their uniform and just walk into the sea."

CHAPTER 3.

Quickly Seize Opportunities

Christina Womack: Nitpicking in NOLA
Shelly Molaschi: Style Consultant

You're going through life and suddenly, you hit a wall. There's something you need to do, or want, and it's nowhere to be found. You know you're not the only person who needs this and it just seems so obvious. This is a light-bulb moment: when the need for a business or service seems brilliantly clear. It might be in your family... or in your clothes closet. Each sparked a new business for these entrepreneurs.

Nitpicking in Nola

When Christina Womack brought her four young kids for their back-to-school haircuts, the hairdresser had bad news.

All four children — adorable in every other way! — were infested with head lice.

Anyone whose kids have had lice knows what an enormous amount of aggravation is involved in getting rid of them (the lice, that is!).

You have to buy the toxic, foul-smelling shampoo from the drugstore, comb the nits out of the kids' hair, wash everything they've used or sat on, and dry everything at a high temperature. Then you walk on eggshells for the next few days, thinking every time you feel the slightest itch that the lice have come back and you've got them, too.

This would be a lot for anyone. But as it happened, Christina was also nine months pregnant when the crisis erupted. And her husband was leaving on a business trip the next day.

"So, we were really freaked out about the whole thing," Christina recalls. "And I was pregnant, so I knew I couldn't use anything toxic. And I also had a child whose asthma wasn't under control at the time. The pharmacist told me. 'You really can't use anything over the counter, because he will have an asthma attack.'"

Christina did have a couple of things going for her. She had a major deadline, in the due date of her fifth child. And she has training as a paralegal.

"Being a paralegal, I know how to research. And so I researched the CDC (Centers for Disease Control), not mom blogs. I went to people who knew what they were talking about. I talked to entomologists. And I got it out."

The kids were lice-free. But still … there was that itchy feeling in her own hair.

Three days after giving birth, Christina flew to Houston to have her head checked, because it was the closest place where professionals provided the service.

"I didn't have (lice), but I needed that warm, fuzzy feeling to know I didn't have it. And I realized that there needed to be something like that, not just in New Orleans but in Louisiana," she says.

Thus, was hatched Nitpicking in NOLA, which now employs a team of trained professionals who will come to your home or school — in discreet, unmarked vehicles — and treat your family and everything around you for lice, while providing guidance on keeping the critters at bay.

Founded in 2009, the business is booming. Christina estimates she has personally combed through the hair of 5,000 to 6,000 children, but she's not going it alone: She's got 10 independent contractors and is expanding to the Gulf Coast.

"There are two types of clients," she says. "Ones that have done it themselves — they've gone to the drugstore, picked up the medication and done the treatment —and they're just not sure they've gotten everything out, so they'll call us and say can you come double-check our work? And we'll do that.

"We have other parents who don't want to touch it. They want nothing to do with it. So they call us and we start the process and finish it. We handle everything that needs to be done: the combing, the treatment."

While parents may have a lot of questions about lice — Where did they come from? How do we get rid of them? Why must children in preschool play with hats? — one question that seems low on the list is price. I've asked four or five mothers who hired nitpickers, and none of them knew, or apparently cared to know, what it cost.

Christina acknowledges that desperate parents often announce, "I don't care what it costs." But, she stresses, it's way more affordable than you might think — from $100 to $200, depending on how many people need to be treated.

Before the interview I spoke with two former customers who actually didn't have a clue how much they paid for the service. In economic terms, the demand is "inelastic"—price is not a big factor. (OK, this is the last nerdy economic jargon in the book!) "I think I just tied my daughter to a chair in the driveway, went to Starbucks, ordered myself a Frappuccino, returned, and wrote that nice lady a check." I hope she was kidding.

Christina is expanding the business to the Gulf Coast. That means she's taking on new contractors, who shadow her on the job to learn both the science and the art of nitpicking.

"Training takes time," she says. Besides the treatment, it's about "how you calm a crying mother or what to do with a dad who is about to shave someone's head. That's the joy I get out of it, bringing everybody down from Defcon 1," aka imminent nuclear war.

Lice have been associated with being dirty, but that's not the case, she says. Christina compares lice infestations to strep throat, or a cold. And grownups are not exempt.

"It's typically moms who end up with it. Dads don't. I think the science behind it is that dads don't love their children as much," Christina deadpans.

"Or it could be that typically women have longer hair."

Shelly Molaschi, Style Consultant

When you think about it, there's no real need for human beings to wear clothes. Skin is waterproof! We don't absolutely need to live where it's too cold to survive without a winter coat. In most places we could do just fine naked.

As interesting an idea as that might be, every human society on earth wears some sort of clothing. Americans spend 4 percent of their budget on clothing (compared to 11 percent on food). Our closets are crammed. So why is it that so often, it feels like we have nothing to wear?

This is where Shelly Molaschi comes into the picture. Shelly is a style coach who uses the training she gained as a television news anchor and reporter to help other people get dressed — with what's in their closet already.

(This is in contrast to my industry, radio — an industry that is notorious for being poorly dressed.)

We wear 20 percent of the clothes in our closets over and over again, Shelly says, because we're in a rut, we get comfortable and we don't know how to change it up.

In television, "they bring consultants in and they say here's how to dress, how to do your hair, your makeup. ... I take what I've learned, and I show you how to do that in your own closet. You have everything you need, I promise you," she says.

Having someone peer into your closet and advise you what to wear might be an idea most people have never considered. I sort of envisioned Shelly storming into a closet full of clothes hangers and going all Joan Crawford on them.

She laughed and assured me there's nothing to be afraid of.

"People kind of think, 'Well, what's a style coach?' But our friends have been getting into our closets with us and helping us get dressed, for dates, and for weddings, forever," she points out. "I'm that friend. I'm that person who can get into your closet and help you get dressed. ... I say, 'You've already done this! Your bestie is here!'"

This got me thinking. Many of us have clothes that no longer fit, probably because we have put on a few pounds. Do we keep them? I had a friend named Bill who always made me laugh because in his very big house, he had a *Fat Bill* closet and a *Skinny Bill* closet.

"Everybody has that closet," Shelly tells me. "It's called the 'before' closet. Before the baby, before the divorce, before the 20 pounds. We keep it. And it's such a pain point in our life! Do you really need to visit that every single morning when you get dressed?

"It definitely is one of the five steps we do in your closet: getting rid of the 'before' closet. It does not serve you."

But isn't it hard to tell someone that the clothes they bought, presumably in their right minds, don't look good on them anymore?

This is where I learned that in her business as a style coach, Shelly is also a little bit of a psychiatrist.

"They already know," she says. "When they put something on and I look at them and I say, 'How do you feel in that?' They already know.

"I say, 'Take it off! It's not a tattoo!

"It's clothes!'"

Peter's Principles #3

As my mother would say: "If everyone took their problems and placed them on a table, you would look around and take yours back." You're not alone. Every other entrepreneur is facing difficulties in running and growing their businesses. Talk to them. You'll often find that theirs are worse than yours. And they have answers to your troubling issues.

CHAPTER 4.

Realize Your Worth and Abilities

Desiree Ontiveros: Badass Balloon Co.
Todd Wackerman: STEM Library Lab
Paco Robert: Dinner Lab

You have more skills than you might realize. Do you love to plan parties? Maybe, like one of our entrepreneurs here, there's a business in it for you. Do you know the classroom inside out? Educators are especially adept at identifying problems in their field and targeting new businesses to solve them.

Badass Balloon Co.

Desiree Ontiveros has a job she loves, working for herself. That makes sense, because who else would hire her to sell party balloons printed with X-rated slogans?

The owner of Badass Balloon Co. came up with the idea as she helped to plan a friend's bachelorette party a few years back. Desiree wanted to custom-print some of her gang's edgy inside jokes on balloons, but the small batches were too expensive. However, the idea of an adult-themed balloon business intrigued her. Ordering in bulk made the designs affordable, and before long the one-time stylist and publicist was filling requests from all over the world for balloons with sayings like "Drinks Well with Others" "Happy F&$%ing Birthday" and "Let's Party, Bitches!" (and many that are even racier, but you can see them at badassballoonco.com).

That's not all the company sells. There's iridescent confetti, cake toppers, napkins and even novelty pinatas. But the sassy balloons are still among the most popular products.

"I knew that my friends would like it. People like me would like it," Desiree says.

These balloons are tailored to the age of social media. "Most people use them for Instagram props," Desiree says. Photo booths and party backdrops love them. "People just have the best time with them."

She's a serious entrepreneur who did the math to make sure that adult balloons were a viable business idea as well as a fun project she could throw herself into. "We have really good profit margins, which goes back to the fact that we make such large runs," she says. "I pass the savings on to the end user." Because, as the balloon says, "It can't all be champagne, cocaine and hookers!"

After our radio interview at Commander's Palace, Desiree presented me with a generous sample of her work. I then had to exit the fancy dining room carrying a helium balloon that read "Better a year older than a month late!"

Where does she get these hilarious lines? New Orleans, where the company is headquartered, is a perpetual source of inspiration. There's also her own energy and sense of humor.

And then, there's her studio, where she gets some great ideas. A few years back, Desiree and her family found, bought and renovated a 1973 Airstream trailer, her "most prized possession," which now serves as a retro-stylish workshop and headquarters.

"Like all good startup stories, Badass Balloon Co. started in my living room, and when I needed the space, moved to my mom Martha's spare bedroom," Desiree explains on her website.

"Turns out my mom was happy to give up her yard for the Airstream. It meant she was getting back her spare bedroom. And her own bedroom. And laundry room. Oh, and her dining room."

The Airstream, now fixed in place, is a party boat decorated in bright colors where new ideas are hatched.

Other ideas come from that gang of friends. "We've had some pretty fun times," Desiree says. And she keeps her ears open. "People say the darndest things!"

Stem Library Lab

After Hurricane Katrina, New Orleans public schools began morphing into independently run, publicly financed charter schools, then the cutting edge of school reform. New Orleans math and science teacher Todd Wackerman wanted to encourage his students to pursue in-demand careers in science, engineering, technology and math, and was frustrated because there wasn't enough equipment and funding for hands-on experiments in the school where he taught. Todd took a leap and left his job to start the STEM Library Lab of science equipment. It's in New Orleans, and it's the first of its kind anywhere.

The library stocks everything from Bunsen burners to primate skulls, and lots in between. Teacher memberships are free. Schools pay $2,000 to

$3,000 to join, and partial scholarships are available. Compare that to a bill of $65,000 to $110,000 for a fully stocked school science department.

As schools tighten their belts, science often takes a big hit. This, of course, is a terrible decision. The U.S. has become a science-led economic juggernaut, and we're in desperate need of scientists to keep up. You can only learn so much by dropping Mentos in a Diet Coke to create a low-budget geyser!

I'm so glad that Todd and his operation are out there filling this gap. I certainly don't mean to disparage those other classes. But really, how often will you use long division or be asked to draw a map of Mesopotamia?

The library is definitely a wonderland for science geeks. But that's not all.

"We want to solve both the problem of the teacher who says, 'I could teach this great lesson if I had 30 compasses, iron filings and magnets tomorrow!' and they can walk in and get that," Todd says, "or the teacher who says, 'I want to plan my next unit, and it's going to involve the digestive system; can you order me a digestive system model?'"

That's not something you're going to find at Walmart!

One order he told me about included a muscular arm model that comes apart so students can study muscles and bones, cleaning strips for microscope slides, and a bowling ball on a string that can be pushed back and forth for the classic experiment in conservation of momentum.

The library also plans with teachers so that equipment is rotated among schools and available when they need it.

Todd knows that equipment is just one piece of the puzzle for science education in the city's schools.

"The fact that teachers can't get the cool stuff that they need for their classroom is a big deal," he says. But he also wants to supply schools with expertise in planning lessons. To that end, Todd is looking for partnerships with STEM departments in local universities, and the library offers office hours with experts, educators' open houses and supply swaps.

There's always a new idea bubbling in the education business world. And chances are, it will bubble up in New Orleans, still on the front lines of the education revolution.

Dinner Lab

In 2012 we met a guy called Paco Robert. Paco was a Tulane MBA student who came on our show and talked about a business he'd co-founded with a former schoolteacher named Brian Bordainick, a pop-up supper club called Dinner Lab.

People paid from $100 to $200 a year to join, and then were invited to last-minute dinners, generally under $100. The meals were prepared by emerging chefs and hosted in offbeat locations, like empty warehouses dressed up for the evening with candlelight and flowers. Dinners were never in the same place twice.

The idea was to serve up ever-new and exciting dining experiences, while collecting data from diners that could be used to craft the next dinner, or even to market to brick-and-mortar restaurants.

Dinner Lab earned the name because it was an experiment. And it looked like a successful experiment, growing from New Orleans to 33 cities across the nation in three years, attracting millions of dollars from investors and drawing admiring articles in Forbes, the Wall Street Journal and The New York Times.

We spoke to Paco again in 2015. Before Dinner Lab, he'd also started a restaurant and worked as a restaurant consultant. But this was a whole new challenge. In the entrepreneurial world, one of the buzzwords we hear is scale: how a successful idea can grow to make everybody a lot of money. The scaling of Dinner Lab had been nothing short of phenomenal. Every entrepreneur in New Orleans wanted to know the answer to the question: How did they do it? How did they grow to 30 cities in three years?

Paco credited supportive investors and mentorship with helping the enterprise grow quickly. "Having a good group of investors and a good advisory board helped us think through that scalability," Paco said. The company had pulled in more than $10 million in venture capital over three years. "Money is one thing, but what makes a good investor is taking the time and believing in what you are doing. The initial investors were investing in us, not necessarily the business itself." The investors allowed Paco and Brian to bounce ideas around, "throw some stuff at the wall and see what sticks."

Paco said the lab replicated the same process in city after city, plugging in local chefs and locations. The process, however, was supposed to be standard, he said. Keeping the core of their original team allowed the company to take the concept from city to city.

Paco saw a lot to be proud of in Dinner Lab. By attracting a mix of young professionals and empty nesters, the dinners allowed people to meet across generations and social strata. The business counted new friendships and even marriages among its successes.

Dinner Lab also allowed striving up-and-coming chefs to prove their chops in a competitive environment. Some went on to launch their own restaurants.

Still, Paco described Dinner Lab to Forbes in a 2016 interview as a logistical challenge. With so many moving parts in so many cities, the team learned on the fly. With everything new every dinner, there were stumbles. Midnight start times didn't work because so many diners showed up drunk. In New York, fire trucks suddenly surrounded the pop-up when smoke from a propane burner alarmed the neighbors.

Less than a year after our lunch, Dinner Lab suddenly shut down. "It is with a very heavy heart that we have to tell you, but effective immediately, Dinner Lab will be suspending operations and halting events," said a letter posted to social media. The announcement didn't give a reason, but in the interview with Forbes.com, Brian said the business struggled to find a sustainable model. While the investors were as understanding as "humanly possible," the loss of principle was, as always, difficult to manage, he said. Dinner Lab had big ambitions to scale the company, but working with part-time contractors must have made each event feel like opening night at a restaurant.

Paco was a student of mine. He's a great guy. And I loved this dining concept. The company was backed by some very smart investors. My wife and I even joined in on one of their events. Had Dinner Lab been a public company I just might have bought a few shares. But it wasn't. And that was a good thing.

Peter's Principles #4

Be honest with yourself and understand that every choice in life involves some kind of risk/reward tradeoff, and many wonderful ventures end in failure. It's part of the game. A good analogy might be that "capitalism without bankruptcy would be like Christianity without hell."

CHAPTER 5.

The Joy of Making Connections

Jaime Glas: Haute Work
Emily Degan: St. Hugh

Many careers and leisure activities are still dominated by men. Women who join their ranks find opportunities that have been overlooked by those who still think it's a man's world. The vibrant businesses we profile here are great examples of why a diverse class of entrepreneurs can thrive as they observe and meet the demands of a changing workforce.

And, as you see throughout this book, a disproportionate number of the most interesting and successful guests on our show have been women.

HauteWork

Jaime Glas had a problem.

As a young intern in the oil and gas industry, Jaime was required to wear fire-retardant safety gear like everyone else on the jobsite. The coveralls protect workers neck to ankle. But the so-called "unisex" jumpsuits were really tailored for men, and the petite Jaime was swallowed up in the over-sized suits. Coming down the metal stairs on an oil rig, she had to hold up the pants to keep from tripping. It wasn't safe; in fact, it violated a rule that workers keep three points of contact on stairs at all times.

I've seen this problem first-hand. Several years ago, I was touring an offshore structure called LOOP (the Louisiana Offshore Oil Port) with a high-ranking female elected official. To tour the facility, we needed to wear special industrial boots. I still laugh when I remember the call to the lower deck of the rig. "Johnny, do you have those steel toe boots in a women's 6?"

One day, Jaime's boss wanted to meet the intern for dinner right after work. Self-consciously, Jaime shuffled into a Carthage, Texas, restaurant with her pants legs rolled up and fabric sagging from her waist.

"It was sort of embarrassing," she recalls.

But Jaime also had a solution. Today, she heads up HauteWork, a company that creates flame-retardant safety wear tailored to women. When she and I had lunch at Commander's Palace in New Orleans, Jaime brought along an attractive and very safe jumpsuit.

"And that was part of my motivation to do this: to make something you feel comfortable meeting friends after work or to lunch in," she says. (Plus, if the waiter gets crazy with the flaming Bananas Foster, she's prepared!)

Twenty-two percent of workers in the oil and gas industry are women. Not all are working in the field, but many report to an industrial site to do their jobs. Safe clothing that fits them seems like an obvious untapped market, but Jaime was the first, as far as she knows, to offer suitable clothes for women. HauteWork's line of coveralls, shirt and pants comes in sizes extra small to 4X, in seven colors that include not just traditional gray and black, but sage, pink and light blue. When we spoke, Jaime was working on comfy, fire-retardant pajamas and underwear for women who live on oil rigs for weeks-long shifts.

Jaime crowd-sources her ideas in a group of 150 women who work in the industry, looking for more ways to keep women on the job safe and confident about their appearance. The marketing is also geared to women.

"Trunk shows are the big advertising we are doing now," she says. But, "It's really been a lot of word of mouth. Every jumpsuit a woman buys and puts on in the field, on every day, there's probably 20 people she sees."

She took advantage of a downturn in oil and gas to build her company, confident that the cyclical industry would return. The safety gear is also worn by women at chemical plants. She got advice from her mom and other family members, entrepreneurs in their own right who own a popular New Orleans garden center.

At first, most of Jaime's customers were women who were willing to spend almost $200 for a coverall that fit. Now, many companies put in orders for their female employees.

"Some of the downstream plants (like refineries) around here are more strict about having the safety group purchase FRC (fire-retardant clothes) for the employees," says Jaime, who speaks fluent "oilfield." "What I'm used to, upstream oil and gas (i.e., exploration and production) in Texas, employees can buy them on their own."

It's a great idea, and in hindsight, a pretty obvious unmet need until now. It only took a bright young intern to see it, during her first days at work.

Jaime acknowledges that major industrial clothing manufacturers have jumped in with women's FRC lines in the past couple of years, and even offered to buy her out. But she thinks her women-first branding appeals to her customers.

"We only are making women's clothes," Jaime says. "We've never even tried to make something for men. We want to create a product that women want to wear." As she told a competitor, "Why would a woman want to buy something from you when for 100 years you made only clothes for men?"

St. Hugh

In fall, the marshes of Delacroix, Louisiana, turn tawny gold. The autumn sun lights up the tall grasses and shimmers on the water, luring hunters and anglers to the state justly known as a "Sportsman's Paradise."

This is where New Orleans native Emily Degan hunted ducks as a girl with her father, and where she returned, years later, for inspiration when she launched a line of women's hunting clothes, St. Hugh.

(If the name "Delacroix" rings a bell, that might be because it also gets a mention in Bob Dylan's ballad, "Tangled Up in Blue"!)

"Growing up I always had a really hard time finding apparel for hunting that fit right and felt good, not to mention looked good," Emily says.

Women tend to be smaller than men, of course, and need clothes tailored to fit. And Emily told me that women also tend to suffer more from the fierce kick of a shotgun — something she learned early on.

"I enjoyed shooting, but I didn't enjoy the aftereffects of bruising," Emily says. "Women's collarbones protrude more than men's do." (Yet another thing I didn't know about women. Where will it end?)

"That was something I knew I wanted to find protection for," Emily says. So, St. Hugh shooting jackets and vests have ample padding.

Finally, on the theory that when you look your best, you do your best, Emily puts special care into designing field wear that makes a stylish transition from hunting lodge to house party. It's not standard camo. In fact, images of the Louisiana marsh are woven into the pattern of every piece.

"We created our own 'marsh print,'" Emily says. "I took thousands of photos of the marsh grass and terrain down in Delacroix and other places in Southeast Louisiana. I adjusted the coloring to account for seasonality factors, and time-lapsed those photos to come up with a color palette that I used to create our own print."

Painstaking preparation is to be expected from Emily Degan, who graduated from the University of Notre Dame with a degree in accounting. She's a CPA who worked for two years in mergers and acquisitions at Deloitte in Chicago.

While she liked her job, she knew it wasn't something she wanted to do long term. For years, she'd thought about creating a line of women's hunting gear.

"It got to the point where I thought, 'I've always had this idea, so if I don't do it now while I'm young and don't have dependents, it probably isn't going to happen,'" she recalls.

Her business training served her well.

"Before we got started, I did extensive amounts of market research," Emily says. She sifted through U.S. Census data for the Southeast, and cross-referenced it against hunting licenses. She found 3.2 million potential customers in the Southeast — women who hunt or are closely related to someone who hunts.

One thing she didn't have was experience in clothing design or manufacture. But she had taken sewing classes as a girl at Ursuline Academy in New Orleans — classes that, at the time, seemed unconnected to any future she had planned. Thanks to those basic skills, though, Emily was able to craft technical designs for the clothing, which she handed off to a patternmaker.

The clothes are manufactured in the United States. This is something of a rarity these days, and Emily is very proud of it.

Sales of St. Hugh — the name is a nod to St. Hubert, patron saint of hunters — are about 50-50 between hunters and non-hunters, Emily says. She promotes the gear at wildlife and fisheries events, hunt clubs and trade shows, hoping to grow the market for a sport she loves.

"Exposing more women to this really fun activity is definitely part of our mission," she says.

Peter's Principles #5

Don't hesitate to ask for help. Friends and family are usually more than happy to lend a hand. But select these friends wisely. As my family always said, "A friend will help you move a sofa. A good friend will help you move a body."

CHAPTER 6.

Learn To Go With the Flow

Wingate Jones: Southern Costume Company

Andre Champagne: Hollywood Trucks

They say if you love your work, it won't feel like work. Do you have a pastime you're passionate about? An expertise others could learn from? Those are the places where successful small businesses are born.

Southern Costume Company

Wingate Jones remembers the first time he fitted an actor for a costume.

He was 17, working in his father's theatrical wardrobe business in Hollywood, California. The customer: none other than the famous (and famously rotund) actor Orson Welles.

"He was big as a house, sitting in a chair," Wingate recalls. By this time, he'd already spied stars like John Wayne and international sex symbol Gina Lollobrigida in the halls of the business, Western Costume Company. "But they're people, just like you and I, and they're to be treated with respect." His father's motto: "Treat others as you would have them treat you."

That time-honored rule carried Wingate through many professional changes as he moved up in the costume business, moved to New Orleans, created an entirely new successful career as an IT manager and finally made the leap to start his own local wardrobe business, Southern Costume Company.

"One thing led to the other and I thought, if I open up a shop, I'll see some of these people that are coming in, that are my peers and my friends," people he'd worked with in California. And, "it would be a great opportunity to provide a service to the productions coming in."

Southern Costume is dedicated to serving the movie companies that flocked to Louisiana thanks to a state film tax credit program, which made shooting in the Pelican State economically competitive. But while the finances were inviting, the infrastructure to make films was lacking.

Wingate's business aims to supply productions with the Class A, production-ready wardrobe goods they had a hard time finding far from Hollywood. Southern Costume worked with big productions such as "Treme," "Dallas Buyers Club," "12 Years a Slave" and "21 Jump Street."

The business offers costume rentals for special occasions and manufactures costumes for Mardi Gras courts and parades. This is a big market. New Orleanians will dress up in costume for just about any occasion. Based on my observation of a great many events, I firmly believe that a large portion of the city's residents have a nun's habit in their closets. Maybe it's for an impromptu street parade or perhaps just to be on the safe side in case the Pope swings by. It's that kind of town.

The sprawling warehouse-style Southern Costume, located in downtown New Orleans, offers space for wardrobe design and storage, private office space, fitting rooms and retail production supplies. Seamstresses are on duty. It is a team approach.

My first question was logistical. When Wingate needs hundreds of costumes, everything from pirates to vampires, where does he find them all?

"Sometimes we take the free time we have during the summer or our down time and we'll supplement our stock with things we don't already have," he says. "We'll supplement by making things, or I'll go out and buy things I think will add to that collection." If he knows a company is coming to town and needs wardrobes, "we get a script. We read the story, and we find out what the needs are."

All costumes are not created equal. Below Class A are the "passable" Class B costumes. Class C are the costumes sold in a bag for under $100 and used perhaps once. "I've experimented with that market, and at the end of the day, that's not who we are. We're a higher-end shop," Wingate says. But, he adds, "I think we're affordable."

Catering to the vision that a production company has for a film isn't always easy.

Filmmakers often have a very precise idea of what they want costumes to look like. For made-to-order costumes, the most demanding clients are those who know exactly what they want, Wingate says. Sometimes, the wardrobe company knows that a costume just isn't going to look right. In those cases, relationships are key. "The hardest part is developing a relationship that's secure enough where, without coming out and saying that looks horrible, there's enough simpatico there to say this is not going to work, and perhaps this will work better."

Southern Costume experienced some tough times. The film tax credit program was changed, and changed again, by state lawmakers. Filming ground nearly to a halt during the coronavirus pandemic. But it's made a strong comeback. In the many movies and TV shows shot in New Orleans since

Hurricane Katrina, you'll often see the company's stock, worn by actors skinny, rotund and in-between, on the sound stages of Hollywood South.

Hollywood Trucks

Starting your own business is a journey. For Andre Champagne, that journey began in a Honda Civic loaded with all his worldly possessions, chugging across the country from Louisiana to seek his fortune in Hollywood.

Andre is a guy from Napoleonville who thought about going back into the region's famed sugar cane business. But he had just graduated from Louisiana State University, and first he wanted to try his luck in the movie capital of the world.

Once in Hollywood, Andre found work largely on the business side of things, dealing with contracts and logistics. He was determined that one day he would own his own studio. But fortune called – and it called him back to his home state, when Louisiana created generous tax credits to encourage the production of films, commercials and TV shows.

The credits, then upwards of 30 percent, drew filmmakers to Louisiana like flies to honey. Before long, the state earned the nickname "Hollywood South." The trouble was, when film crews got to the Bayou State, there were no stage sets, prop warehouses or other support services — none of the technical support that surrounds the dream-makers of Hollywood.

All tax incentives are controversial. In a strictly accounting sense they look like money losers for the state or municipalities offering them up. But, if you factor in the new ancillary jobs and additional sales tax they bring in (the so-called ripple effect) these breaks often calculate as a significant positive for a region's economy.

"We had a fantastic (tax) program, but no infrastructure," Andre says. Services were being imported at tremendous cost from other states.

Andre had fully expected to stay in California, which he loved, but "I saw this vanguard opportunity" in Louisiana, he says. "I knew nothing about transportation, but I knew it was a substantial line item."

He turned to his family and friends for help to get started.

"I bought seven trucks. I thought if I wanted to ask my friends and family to invest I would make it an asset that could be moved," in case the industry moved.

Andre seized the proverbial "first mover advantage" and quickly expanded his fleet of trucks.

The company grew like crazy as the film industry snapped up tax credits. For a while, it seemed like every time you turned down a street in New Orleans there'd be no place to park, with the curbs completely lined by giant film trucks.

In 2012, Hollywood Trucks was named one of Inc. Magazine's fastest-growing American companies. Besides state-of-the-art equipment, Andre wanted an eco-friendly fleet, and he designed toxin-free talent trailers powered by solar panels. This was a particularly attractive feature to the A-List actors and actresses inhabiting these mobile lairs. By 2015, Andre ran almost 400 vehicles, was expanding into neighboring states, and had partnered with an Atlanta company that gave him the opportunity to grow into Europe and China.

With that kind of success, buyout offers were inevitable. In 2020, Andre sold Hollywood Trucks to Base Camp Inc., another Louisiana movie transportation company.

With creative thinkers like these, you never know what's next. A successful entrepreneur can be counted on to keep looking for new opportunities.

Peter's Principles #6

You don't have to scale, and many of our guests have determined that they are happy and want to stay at their current size and structure. But, if you want to expand, you'll probably need additional money to grow the business.

We've had guests who started by maxing out their credit cards or borrowing against the equity in their homes. More than one guest has joked that their initial funding came from "the three F's" (family, friends and fools).

Some of the more attractive businesses might have the option of raising capital by selling portions of the company to venture capitalists or private equity investors. This requires giving up a piece of your company. And bank loans can come with restrictions on how you can run and expand your business.

There are few Medicis out there handing out free capital.

And securing funding might not be your biggest problem. Scaling requires letting go. You need to find the right people to handle the blocking and tackling while you work on the big picture. My guests often mention this as the most difficult part of running their business. Finding these people can be tough

CHAPTER 7.

You Call the Shots

Ann Parnes: Match Made in NOLA
Leigh and Casey Isaacson: Dig

If what you learned about matchmakers can be sung to the score of "Fiddler on the Roof," you are way behind the times. These days, busy people are turning to professional matchmakers to help them find that special someone. Online dating apps work for some people, but for others, who want more discretion or less scrolling, a human guide can make all the difference. Or, what about narrowing your field down to people who love animals, are kind-hearted and are not too concerned about a little dog hair on the couch? A specialized dating app pairs up folks who want a partner to fit their "dog-forward" lifestyle.

Match Made In NOLA

Arranged marriages might seem odd in the United States, but they're not unusual in some countries. I once had a student who came into our suite to share that his father had just chosen a wife for him. He was thrilled.

After he left, my office mate turned to me and announced that he wouldn't let his own dad pick out so much as a suit for him.

As it turned out, the bride was brilliant, beautiful and very funny. The skeptical colleague later asked if perhaps the father could find a match for him. "I've been hanging around bars for years," he sighed, "and never met a woman like that."

Of course, during the mask-wearing pandemic it got worse. You could have met someone and gotten their number without even knowing if they had teeth.

So, romance is complicated, and for some lovelorn modern singles, the answer might be an old-fashioned one: professional matchmaking.

Ann Parnes has based a business on her knack for finding people who are right for each other. "I've always enjoyed doing it, probably as far back as fifth grade," she tells me.

Nowadays, her process is more sophisticated than passing a note under a desk ("He likes you!"). But it still relies on a personal touch.

She recruits through networks of contacts. "I've also gathered a large database of people who want to be considered as matches. ... I stalk LinkedIn and Facebook and every other social media," she says. Then, "I just arrange a lot of coffees."

Many of her clients have tried online dating sites without success. Then there are those who use ancestry.com as a dating site! Let's not go there.

Of the dating sites, Ann says, "It takes a lot of time and energy, and you have to be OK with rejection. And many times people get frustrated, because the person they think they're meeting looks completely different or sounds completely different than what they are expecting."

That's one reason Ann meets the candidates before she pairs them off. (This is important, because people tend to pad their attributes when describing themselves online.)

Ann gets feedback from clients on how matches went. Some need coaching — and isn't that the kind of thing you always wished you had when you were 18 years old?

"There are other people who keep choosing kind of the same type of partner again and again," Ann says. "So we work with them on figuring out who that partner is and why they are doing that — and to spot them at the outset and avoid them, if that's what they want to do."

For a lot of people, political differences are a deal-breaker. Not every couple can be James Carville and Mary Matalin! For others, the problem might be communication.

"I can't always predict chemistry, but I haven't had any terrible date stories," Ann says.

I asked Ann whether she sometimes meets a potential client and thinks, "This is really a long shot! I'm going to charge them a lot!"

No, she's way nicer than that.

"If I don't think they're going to be successful," she says diplomatically, "I'll just tell them I don't think it's a good time for us to work together. Because that's the worst thing in this business, to overpromise and under-deliver. It kind of keeps you up at night, when someone's heart is on the line."

Dig

When Casey Isaacson brought her toy poodle mix along on a date with her new boyfriend, there were issues. The guy liked Casey, but he didn't like dogs. In fact, he didn't want Layla (known to her family as "the world's cutest dog") in his apartment. It soon became apparent that this relationship could not be saved.

That's how Casey and her sister, Leigh, got the bright idea to start the New Orleans-based dating app Dig, for people who love dogs. (I kind of thought it was a dating app for dogs at first! I told my own dog about it, and he was so thrilled!) And it turns out dog folks are a sizable demographic: 55 percent of single people have a pet.

What's so great about dog owners? Well, they tend to be empathetic people, Leigh points out. But they're also more athletic than non-dog owners, and according to the company's research, they may even live longer. "Basically, everyone should be looking for a dog person," Leigh says.

And dog owners have some special advantages on dating apps. "Guys are seen as 24 percent sexier when they are holding a dog in a picture, compared to when that same person is not," explains Leigh.

Of course that gave me, as a former single guy, an obvious idea: What's to stop someone from borrowing a cute dog for his 24 percent sexier dating profile?

"This is a big problem," Leigh admits. That's why Dig does not require singles to actually own a dog. You just have to like them.

"On our app you have to say whether you have a dog or you do not have a dog," Leigh says. Dig encourages people without dogs to sign up, as long as they know that everyone they meet on the site wants a dog-friendly lifestyle. "Maybe you want to have a dog in the future!" she says, optimistically.

And there's much to learn about a person when you see them interact with their dog, Leigh says. Did he bring a poop bag? ("That's HUGE," she says.) Does he use a choke collar? ("For the dog, that is!")

Leigh has such an interesting background. She earned her master's degree in homeland security and emergency response management from Tulane in 2017 and holds a BA in journalism from Syracuse University. She's been a television reporter in the United States and Namibia. Now, Leigh teaches master's level classes in media, terrorism and disasters at Tulane. She brings all this analytical, research-driven thought to her dating app. Lucky dogs!

Inevitably, large, established industry leaders in the online dating world are looking hard at Dig. "Part of our game plan is to work with some of these bigger companies in the future," Leigh says. Dig is also partnering with companies that serve pet owners, like chow makers and pet stores. "There are opportunities for dog companies to work with us on a lot of different levels." In fact, if you are planning a dog-friendly date, the app will help you out by suggesting the services of those companies, who pay Dig for advertising.

Dig is continuing to move into new cities, offering singles a way to find others who want a dog-forward lifestyle.

Peter's Principles #7

Remember to take care of yourself. After all, you're the company's most valuable asset. Find a way to get away once in a while — I mean a real disconnect from work. "Working vacation" is an oxymoron, like tight slacks, Dodge Ram or fun run.

CHAPTER 8.

Be Your Own Boss

Hansel Harlan: Marsh Dog
Simone Bruni: Demo Diva

Doing well by doing good: That's the mantra of many of today's entrepreneurs. Not only are you starting a business, often you are benefiting your community with needed jobs and services, or solving important problems.

Marsh Dog

The toughest job in America would be taking a census count of the invasive, water-loving nutria.

Millions of these incredibly prolific rodents, originally from South America, have ravaged Louisiana's marshlands, chewing through every green thing in their path and allowing the stripped land to wash away. An explosive birth rate – three litters a year, six to eight nutria per litter – swiftly outpaces the efforts of trappers.

Louisiana lawyer Hansel Harlan learned about nutria as a graduate student in Argentina, the creatures' native land. He'd always assumed they were indigenous to Louisiana. But in fact, they'd been brought to the state in the 1930s and bred here in captivity for their soft, luxuriant pelts. Then they escaped and found the warm Louisiana marsh a year-round haven where they reproduced "like rabbits on steroids," as Hansel puts it. The documentary "Rodents of Unusual Size" tells the strange and rather frightening story.

Eventually, animal fur fell out of favor in the market, and they weren't worth trapping for pelts. State conservationists grew desperate.

"They tried to turn it into food for human consumption some time back, when they were initially trying to figure out how to tackle the problem of overpopulation," Hansel says. Recipes for nutria were developed and began to appear on the menus of fine restaurants under their fancy French name, Ragondin. Diners weren't fooled for long. They lost their appetite once they got a look at what they were eating – a hefty, oversized rat with a hairless tail and curving orange teeth.

When you didn't tell people where the meat came from, they thought it was great. When you told them, though, they ran away and threw up.

But you know who doesn't care where their dinner comes from? Dogs, that's who. Hansel's Marsh Dog cooked up treats from ground nutria, in flavors that apparently drive dogs wild. They're low-fat and high protein, and veterinarians recommend the products for dogs who have developed allergies to commercial feed.

Nutria seems highly addictive for the canine set. I brought home a couple of Hansel's biscuits for my dog, Lucky, and he acted like it was the best thing he'd ever tasted in his entire life. In fact, he was obsessed and became so insistent that my wife jokingly told me, "Don't you ever bring that 'dog crack' back into the house!"

I spoke to Hansel over lunch at Commanders, with some tempting-looking nutria jerky and dog biscuits on the table between us. (Commander's was a great sport about this unauthorized appetizer.) It happened that my other guest that day was Arthur Matherne, an old friend who runs Airboat Tours by Arthur out of Des Allemands, Louisiana.

Arthur takes guests out to see the beautiful marsh. A highlight of the tours is a visit with Big Al, a giant alligator. Occasionally Arthur will offer Al some nutria meat. But often, it's no use. The gator turns up its giant green snout at the swamp critter. It's like Al is saying, "Nutria AGAIN?" Even the predators are tired of them.

Arthur said, regretfully, that while he often sees as many as 100 "nutria rats" scuttling away from the airboat as it roars through the marsh, the critters are hardly worth trapping any more and the state bounty of $6 a tail left the fur and meat to rot. That caught Hansel's attention! By the end of the meal, Marsh Dog had a lead on a new source of cheap nutria, and the marsh had taken another step toward recovery.

Hansel hoped that if demand for Marsh Dog treats grew, the state wouldn't have to spend the $2 million a year it was laying out on the bounty program, which, even with a goal of 400,000 trapped nutria a year, barely kept the pests in check.

"This is money the state could use for other things," like building levees or planting trees to restore the marsh, he says.

Give dogs a quality treat, save the state money and save the wetlands. Hansel's business idea was a win-win-win for us, and a lose-lose-lose for those ravenous rodents.

At the end of 2020, Hansel announced that Marsh Dog would close down, because, he said, he couldn't fulfill the growing national demand. That might have been the smartest good-bye ever, because in June 2021, the company was purchased for an undisclosed amount by Chasing Our Tails, a national pet-food manufacturer based in Minnesota.

Demo Diva

We often hear inspiring stories about entrepreneurs who take a crazy chance on something, and it pays off. But no story is more inspiring than Simone Bruni's.

Simone was an event and party planner in New Orleans. And then, in August 2005, Hurricane Katrina hit and the federal levee system that was supposed to protect New Orleans failed, causing 80 percent of the city to flood. The party was over.

In the words of former Chicago mayor Rahm Emanuel, "a disaster is a terrible thing to waste." Simone made a fast pivot into a new line of work. (When possible, make a legal U-Turn.)

"People were asking us to help gut their houses," she recalls. "And from gutting their houses, then they said they'd decided on a demolition."

From knowing nothing about demolition, Simone waded into what was not just a male-dominated but a male-only world, and used that as her entrée. She put on a hardhat and painted her dumpsters bright pink, and Demo Diva was born. Today, the company is a multi-million dollar demo business. Its Pepto-Bismol-colored trash bins are a familiar sight around New Orleans, and the company is expanding to nearby states.

No one was more surprised than Simone.

"I thought I would be a flash in the pan and gone," she says. "All I owned was a name: Demo Diva." But, she says, "It just snowballed."

"There wasn't a master plan," she says. "There wasn't a business plan. There wasn't even a one-year plan!"

Simone chose the name "Demo Diva" and the trademark pink color to appeal to women.

"I thought women were the only ones who would trust me, or give me a chance," Simone says. But everyone needed her service. "It was an entire 'disasterized' community."

Out of that tough time was born a successful business, one Simone quickly grew to love as she aided the rebirth of New Orleans after the flood. A lot of people inside and outside of the city had their doubts, and a friend of mine called it "the greatest comeback since Lazarus." Who could argue with that?

"The blessing was to be a viable part of rebuilding New Orleans," Simone says.

In recent years, Simone's business has taken a logical step forward into salvaging architectural elements from the older homes her business has dismantled. That new line of work fits right in with Simone's love of the special community where she lives, by helping unique treasures to (literally) find new homes.

A small business isn't just about making bank — although that's an important part! For many small business people, their ventures are also about doing good in the world. Following your heart can be a way to follow the money.

Peter's Principles #8

The #1 issue facing businesses is labor. Finding the people you want is a difficult and time-consuming task. Re-training new personnel is expensive, so you need to find some way to "put a little glue in the seat" (i.e. getting them to stay on). I heard this from an HR consultant. I just love this expression.

Delegating additional responsibilities and developing a plan for advancement that would lead to higher wages are the simplest first step. When you lose an employee, be sure to sit down and have an exit interview with them. The feedback may be invaluable for tweaking your operations or management style.

CHAPTER 9.

Create Jobs

Scott Wolfe Sr.: Melba's
John Blancher: Rock'n'Bowl

Laundromats and bowling alleys sound like retro Americana institutions that have faded into the past. But with imagination and hard work, two New Orleans entrepreneurs made them hip — and profitable.

Melba's

Scott Wolfe Sr. was a successful real estate developer in New Orleans, but one piece of property seemed impossible to lease. A former dry cleaner's in a declining neighborhood, it stood at a busy intersection in the city's Eighth Ward. Not knowing what else to do with it, Scott and his wife, Jane, decided to open a po-boy shop there, peddling the iconic loaded sandwiches on crusty French bread 24/7 to hungry locals, tourists and night owls. The business took off, and today Melba's Old-School Po-Boys is a landmark between the French Quarter and the Lower Ninth Ward, known as widely for its quirky marketing and in-house laundromat as for its New Orleans comfort food.

Scott has a talent for marketing. At age 20, with a loan from his family, he took over a small local grocery store called Wagner's and eventually grew it to 10 locations with the slightly racy motto "You Can't Beat Wagner's Meat." He sold the business in 2003, but the slogan is still seen on bumper stickers in New Orleans. "I guess that will be on my tombstone," Scott says, only a little rueful.

Scott gives much of the credit for the business' success to his wife, Jane. He says he handles the bottom line but "she's the double bottom line. She's the social component of our marriage, and also of our business."

Jane turned her attention to the struggling neighborhood where Melba's is located, and pastor Corey Hicks came along at just the right time. "He came to Melba's one day, introduced himself, told me what he did. We told him we had a business across the street and invited him to use it as a reach-out center for the neighborhood." Today, Hicks' Vine Community Center is located there, and Melba's partners with the pastor on neighborhood toy drives and youth programs.

Besides old-school New Orleans comfort food, Melba's is known around town for the laundromat on the premises. "People in the restaurant don't realize there's a laundromat next door," Scott says. "But in the laundromat, people know there's a restaurant next door," and they'll head over for a sandwich while the clothes spin. Walls covered with art give the place a busy, cheerful vibe. "It's a visual attack," Scott says.

All the marketing efforts are very intentional. Melba's is "a landmark, it's a brand," Scott says. "It took us 20 years to grow Wagner's into a local icon. This one, we kind of speed-tracked it because of the marketing knowledge we had attained. A lot of people don't do that. They take the slow road, they rely on word of mouth."

A sign out in front of Melba's brags that they sell more po-boys than any place on the planet. Of course, po-boys are nearly exclusively sold and eaten in south Louisiana. So there's that. But I believe the guy is a marketing genius.

Another plus for Melba's is the experienced local staff. In a business that sees a lot of turnover, Melba's retains great employees. In fact, after Hurricane Katrina scattered New Orleanians to the winds, Scott and Jane worked hard to locate former staff to bring them to work at Melba's. The head cook, "Mama" Lois Thomas, had relocated to Houston. "We knew we had to find Lois," Scott said. "She's from the Ninth Ward; she's a phenomenal cook and a phenomenal person." Scott tracked her down and heard her out as she said she'd settled in Texas, had gotten married. "Well," he told her, with his typical humor, "you'll have to divorce that guy."

Whatever it took, Mama Lois came back to New Orleans and runs the kitchen at Melba's today, feeding everyone that walks in the door with love.

Is there an entrepreneurship gene? Scott Wolfe Jr., the son of Jane and Scott, started a software company called Levelset to streamline financial records such as cash flow and payments for contractors. This kind of stuff is the bane of that industry, and the business grew quickly. At last check, Levelset was valued at about $500 million. Business success within families isn't uncommon, but is it nature or nurture?

And it doesn't always happen. One guest, a serial entrepreneur, couldn't get either of his children interested in starting a business. He joked, "People say the apple doesn't fall from the tree. But sometimes that apple just rolls, and rolls and ..."

Rock'n'Bowl

New Orleans and Lafayette, Louisiana, might not seem to have a lot in common. Lafayette is a small city with an oil and gas-based economy that's the cultural capital of Acadiana. New Orleans is an international destination, wellspring of music and food, home of the New Orleans Saints, and the site of landmarks like Bourbon Street.

But I remember slide guitar legend Sonny Landreth talking at one concert about Lafayette and New Orleans being sister cities, and in some sense, I think they are.

What these places have in common is an intangible spirit that prioritizes love of life over almost everything else. And something else they have in common: Rock'n'Bowl, the bowling alley, live music venue and event space that was born in New Orleans, survived Hurricane Katrina and is now thriving in both cities.

First of all, is this the best idea ever, or what? The relaxed family vibe of a bowling alley meets the energy of live music and dancing at Rock'n'Bowl every day. A commitment to hosting fundraisers serves the community, while also acting as important marketing outreach, bringing in diverse groups of coworkers, neighbors and schoolmates. And it's a great place for birthday parties!

Rock'n'Bowl was the brainchild of John Blancher, a true believer in many ways. He believes in the power of family, hard work and his Catholic faith to accomplish the seemingly impossible.

John bought the bowling alley in 1988, when it was just a run-down spot in a strip shopping center in New Orleans. He got the idea to add live music to the scene, and before long, it was a favorite hangout of the city's hip nightclubbing crowd.

"One of the advantages I had was that I knew nothing about bowling," John quips, as the once-popular pastime has faded into near-obscurity. "People in the business said 'this can't work.'"

But when he bought the dilapidated business, "I didn't see a bowling alley. I saw a great catering hall that had bowling lanes."

Live music wasn't even part of the formula to start with. "I saw people having bands there with parties, but not bands on a regular basis." Soon, though, he realized how popular the music nights were, and added bands regularly.

John has created a New Orleans institution. When I'm showing off New Orleans to out-of-towners, a few frames at Rock'n' Bowl and the obligatory visit to a drive-through daiquiri shop are a must.

John's faith was tested when levees in New Orleans collapsed in Hurricane Katrina, flooding the city. Blancher had evacuated to Lafayette, near his mother's hometown.

"We had family, and there was beer and wine," says John, speaking as a true New Orleanian.

He watched from Lafayette as the disaster unfolded in the Crescent City. In 2005, Rock'n'Bowl was on the second floor, but the shopping center where it was located flooded, and electricity was out all over the city. In the weeks and months to come, it was a battle to secure skilled labor and parts to rebuild. But with the help of his family and close friends, Blancher returned to business before almost anything else in the flooded parts of New Orleans. Pianist Eddie Bo played for the first post-Katrina opening night. Hundreds of New Orleanians showed up, eager for a break from the hard, dirty work of rebuilding.

Due to a series of business decisions by his family and others, a new opportunity was unfolding down the street from Rock'n'Bowl even as obstacles emerged at the old location.

The family revived an iconic restaurant called Ye Olde College Inn, purchased nearby real estate and eventually moved Rock'n'Bowl to the complex – lock, stock and bowling pins.

Meanwhile, an opportunity was beckoning in Cajun country, the family's Katrina evacuation haven, where John had the feeling his concept of live music and family fun might thrive.

"I've never been welcomed anywhere like I have been in Lafayette. All smiles, energetic, and willing to help," John says.

So in 2017, Rock'n'Bowl opened its second location in Lafayette.

Nowadays, Rock'n'Bowl and Ye Olde College Inn in New Orleans anchor a block of businesses and real estate in a thriving area. The Lafayette business continues to grow. What's next for this family of serial entrepreneurs? Set up the pins, get a beer and see what happens.

Peter's Principles #9

I have my principles. And if you don't like them, well, I have others.

-Groucho Marx

Hmmmn, it's clear that Groucho would not have been a very good business owner. All you really have is your reputation. It takes a lifetime to build and just one unethical decision to destroy.

You're the face of your business — its persona. People want to know that you're a local, responsible, hard-working business builder and creator of jobs, with the best interests of your community in mind.

You are the business. Sheer force of (often very big) personalities can often be instrumental in the success of an enterprise.

And as the owner of a successful business you should be prepared to tell your story – why you opened the doors in the first place.

CHAPTER 10.

Control Your Destiny

Lauren Thom: Fleurty Girl
Jennifer Johns: Pang Wangle

Starting a business in your living room with your tax refund sounds like a cliché. But there's a kernel of truth in many a cliché, and in the case of many successful small businesses, that kind of bootstrapping drives the owner to succeed.

Fleurty Girl

While Fortune 500 companies pay a lot of money for advice from business consultants, Lauren Thom is a valedictorian of the "force of personality school of listening to your gut." In 2009, Lauren took her $2,000 income tax refund and opened a T-shirt shop in her home. T-shirt shops get a bad rap in New Orleans – often sporting crass slogans designed to appeal to Bourbon Street tourists – but Lauren had a different idea. She turned the model on its head, selling shirts that targeted locals, marketing insider humor and New Orleans pride, from #WHODAT T-shirts to fleur-de-lis earrings. Now she's got several stores around town.

Lauren admits it was a crazy idea to start with. New Orleans was over-saturated with T-shirt shops, and she had three kids and no actual store-front. Not to be deterred, she moved all three kids into one bedroom and opened her business in the front room of her home.

"We could have paid off our mortgage, or gone on vacation," Lauren says. "But this was the right way to do it: Bootstrap and go."

"Everybody said I was crazy," she admits. "I was working a fulltime job in Baton Rouge. My mother said I was crazy. Now she's my business partner. The day we opened, the rent was due the next day. Your back is up against the wall, and you do what you have to do and you have to be creative."

Lauren had to be innovative to survive in a very crowded field. She did just about everything differently. This includes taking a counterintuitive approach all the way to her philosophy about hiring.

"I think it's important for me not to hire based on retail experience," she says. "I hire based on 'Do you love New Orleans? Can you talk about New Orleans? Can you recommend places to go?'"

"I can teach a girl, or a guy, how to sell a T-shirt, but I can't teach them how to love New Orleans like we do," she says. "It's based on passion. That's why they're going to work the hardest, not just for me, but for the city." Visitors come to have a good time and revel in the unique magic of New Orleans. "We want to be part of that experience," she says.

Customers from out of town might need the backstory on T-shirts fea-turing beloved but long-gone New Orleans institutions, like the iconic drugstore K&B or the former local bakery chain, McKenzie's. Then there's a T-shirt decorated with a crawfish and the slogan, "Don't eat the straight ones!" Customers are baffled if they haven't encountered the tasty crusta-ceans, and they have to ask. "Except for the guys who come in for Southern

Decadence," Lauren amends, referring to the August LGBTQ festival in the French Quarter. "They love that shirt!"

Lauren is known in New Orleans for her frank, uplifting social media presence, which serves as both marketing and inspiration to Fleurty Girl's many fans. "I had no formal training in social media," she admits. "But I think it's all about being organic, being who you are. When I'm going through a negative situation, I try to be positive to try to help others."

What started as a living room T-shirt business has grown to include jewelry and home décor. Lauren buys from a long list of creative people behind those products. The risk she took with her tax return is helping others. And, Lauren says, "That's a great feeling."

Pang Wangle

Jennifer Johns is a former broadcast journalist who regards herself, first and foremost, as a storyteller. In the past few years, her story has had lots of surprises, subplots and cliffhangers. (Louisiana is noted for producing preachers and storytellers. Jennifer made a great career choice. We have enough preachers.)

Today, she's founder and CEO of Pang Wangle, based in Baton Rouge, which makes women's outdoor clothing with safe and effective insect repellent built in. Amid a pandemic lockdown that squashed other companies, Pang Wangle got some well-timed publicity and was able to reframe itself, from travel gear to the ideal clothing for quarantine porch-sitting and self-care. How smart is that?

Now sales are brisk in wraps, pants and hats. The most brilliant product, in my opinion, was the stylish, one-size-fits-all mosquito-repellant scarf. Jen reports it was a best-seller!

But it was a long and winding road, Jen admits.

"I left Channel 4 (TV in New Orleans) and went on maternity leave and then just never went back," she recalls. "But I wasn't very good at sitting still, so I started teaching at Loyola and Tulane – media classes – and I started a video production company. We did a lot of technical videos for companies, explaining things. And we did some brand films, a couple commercials. And I made two documentary films."

Where did the business experience come in, though?

"Really, making a documentary film. By the time you raise the money, hire the crew, and you write the script, it's essentially like starting a small business," Jen says. The only difference: "I made zero money," she laughs.

"I think I was really looking to do something new," she continues. An earlier foray into selling baby gifts online seemed unappealing at this point in her life. "I'm really into being outdoors, and I was looking for a problem to solve. Getting eaten alive by bugs is a problem that we all live with."

Insect shield for clothing fiber was developed for the U.S. military to ward off Lyme disease among recruits. It's now available for licensing. The proprietary military shield lasts for 70 washes, Jen says.

There are a lot of mosquitoes that are very mad at this company!

Much of Jen's success might look like luck. But as they say, "Chance favors a prepared mind." In February 2020, just before the pandemic, Pang Wangle's first products came out. With a lot of inventory on her hands, Jen was exhibiting at a trade show where specialized travel clothing might appeal to adventurers heading around the globe.

Reporters were interested, but by the time the convention was over, it was all COVID, all the time. Traveling was out, but sitting with friends on the porch was suddenly in. And so was insect repellent. The Los Angeles Times and the Washington Post published articles about Jen's clothing line, and suddenly, Pang Wangle was selling its clothing all over America.

Soon, the company's products were prominently featured on a Buzzfeed list of "the 35 most awesome Mother's Day gifts that are 100 percent quarantine-friendly." And sales continue to do well, as Jen plots a move from her laundry room/office to a more official space from which to command her growing company.

She's also hoping to devote more time to Pang Wangle's outdoors blogs and videos, returning to her roots as a storyteller to help the company grow.

"It's out there. I'm trying to take it a little more mainstream. And I'm trying to grow as fast as I can, to stay at the head of the pack," she says. "We've been bootstrapping so far, and we're seeing a lot of growth quickly. We want to keep that momentum."

Peter's Principles #10

Entrenched markets and industries can be upended. But, you'll need to offer something different. Something better.

You'll also need a game plan. While several of my guests admit they were "winging it" when they started out, each and every one of them now wish they had established goals, objectives, timelines and a couple of plan-B options before they opened the doors. Lauren Siegel says that the biggest reason for failure is a lack of willingness to do the research and an inability to listen.

As always, she's right.

CHAPTER 11.

Flexible Work Hours and Locations

Patrick McCausland: Heaven's Pets

Al Hebert: Gas Station Gourmet

When you have a great idea, sometimes it seems like someone should have thought of it already. Caring services for beloved animal companions after they've passed away? Check. A survey of roadside diners by a "gas station MBA"? Maybe so! But these guests really made it happen.

Heaven's Pets

In 2020, Americans spent more than $99 million on their pets. To put that in perspective, that's more than most countries in the world spend on their military. In New Orleans, we keep spending money on our pets even after they've passed on to "cross the rainbow bridge." We're talking about Heaven's Pets, which calls itself a post-life pet care business. It's a joint venture with Stewart Enterprises, a division of Service Corp. International, the largest provider of funeral and cemetery services in the United States.

Based at Lake Lawn Cemetery just outside the New Orleans city limits, Heaven's Pets will arrange a funeral for a departed pet, or they'll simply cremate your pet and give you the ashes in an urn. They also pride themselves on providing free grief services with a counselor, plus memorial tokens like a paw print or lock of fur for the bereaved family.

The business was founded in 2002 by Jennifer and Brian Melius. Formerly in the veterinary field, with a passionate love for animals and a concern for pet owners, the Meliuses felt that death care for pets and their human families was a need that wasn't being met. For three years, the Meliuses held services at their home while using a pet crematory in Baton Rouge. That changed in 2006 when construction was completed on the Heaven's Pets crematorium and memorial gardens outside New Orleans.

On the show, I spoke to Patrick McCausland, president of Heaven's Pets.

The Meliuses "wanted to have more than was being offered," Patrick told me. In particular, they sought grief counseling and private cremations. "People will spend on their pets, but they want to have something in return," Patrick says. So Heaven's Pets offered relief in grief support, plus memorialization options like niches and columbariums. You can get a plaque or a brick in your pet's name, and the beautiful gardens are made available for services and pet blessings during the year.

We love our pets. Often more than humans. I crack up when I think of that line from Jerry Seinfeld "If you see two life forms, one of them is making a poop, the other one's carrying it for him, who would you assume is in charge?" This kind of makes you think, doesn't it?

It might not be legal to dig a hole in the backyard for Fido after he passes away, and really, isn't a hand-carved wooden urn on the mantel nicer? Patrick says that laws for the disposal of animal remains differ across the country, but Heaven's Pets and its parent company are trying to get more consistent regulations passed.

Most of the companion animals cared for by Heaven's Pets are, of course, cats and dogs. But Patrick has handled arrangements for the remains of a pot-bellied pig and even a 150-pound python.

With pets seemingly becoming more closely woven into our lives every day, it's not surprising that this innovative business found its audience. Oh, and during economic downturns, it's been shown that more, not less, money is spent on pets. The $6 latte and the expensive sneakers may be goners. But, Chansey and Mr. Pants will be lavished on. Wall Street sees the pet business as a high growth, recession-resistant business.

Gas Station Gourmet

There is no shortage of colorful personalities in South Louisiana, and there are surprising numbers of people with unique ideas and businesses, but there are very few whose ideas are more unique, or whose personality is more colorful, than Al Hebert's.

Al, otherwise known as the Gas Station Gourmet, lives near the Vermilion River outside Abbeville, Louisiana. By day, Al is a news producer and reporter at a Lafayette TV station, but he also writes a popular column about gas station food for a trade magazine that serves the National Association of Convenience Stores.

The Gas Station Gourmet project also includes TV and online travel articles gasstationgourmet.com). But he got where he is via one of the most eccentric business backgrounds I've ever encountered.

Al started out in the sheriff's office, became a detective — and then a hostage negotiator. Looking to do something a little more low key, he somehow ended up as a TV personality, hosting a cooking segment on the news.

Then one day on assignment he did a story about a gas station in Crowley, Louisiana, and was amazed by the delicious food. And so the persona and the business of Gas Station Gourmet was born.

Al has visited hundreds of convenience stores tucked inside gas stations along highways and byways all over America. By now, he can tell whether he will love the food the minute he walks in. It's all about eye contact. If the people minding the store look him in the eye when they tell him about the food, then lunch is going to be good.

I admit, I was a bit skeptical of gas station food. But Al straightened me out with the line, "C'mon, Pete, we're not talking about Slim Jims and honey buns. This is real food!"

According to Al, small businesses could learn a lot from successful independent gas stations. He calls it a "gas station MBA." Al explains what he meant. "A small business can employ some of the same strategies that a gas station uses."

Faced with Walmart and other corporate giants, gas station owners who thrive today have learned they need to pivot — to offer something different, a little "outside the box."

They might spice their hamburger patties with the seasonings of their homeland in the Mideast, and be eager to talk world politics over the meal. They might offer local specialties, like boudin balls or andouille sausage in South Louisiana, or display a collection of antique toys, like a station owner in Ohio. But they're always eager to chat, and Al says he's met some of the most interesting people behind those gas-station counters.

There's more to the "gas station MBA." Al finds those who do well retain their employees long-term by offering good benefits and flexibility for family events. He says gas stations succeed with high sales volumes and prices that match online vendors. It can work, but "a lot of 'em are afraid to do it," Al says.

There's also a concept called channel blurring — when a store that has a normal or historical line of products introduces something new. "One day this guy in Crowley, he's a convenience store (owner), he gets a brand-new saddle," Al says. "He puts a saddle in the store, marks it up a hundred percent, and a week later it's sold. Now every couple months he sells a saddle!" In another example, he said, "There's a convenience store in Texas where you can buy barbed wire and nails by the pound."

That's it. I'm going to head back over to campus and develop a curriculum based on the Gas Station MBA. I'll be pitching it to our dean as soon as we finish writing this book.

Peter's Principles #11

"The key to being a good manager is keeping the people who hate me away from those that are still undecided."

-Casey Stengel, legendary baseball manager

You may have a great product, a winning smile and an IQ that could boil water, but that's probably not enough. You need to build a cohesive team. Whether it's caring for people in loss, or running an awesome service station, teamwork makes the dream work.

CHAPTER 12.

No Need to Wear Your Best Trousers

Ashley Hauck: No Doody

Brendan Finke, Joe McMenemon: ChapterSpot

Some business ideas are less than glamorous — but highly in demand. Either they're considered "dirty work" or they're just so detail-oriented that most people aren't interested. The fact that many people aren't drawn to these enterprises means there's more opportunity for your new idea.

No Doody

OK. Putting Ashley Hauck and his business on the radio show was a bit of a battle. The show's producer reminded me that "this is a LUNCH SHOW."

Before the chapter on poop, Ashley Hauck's story could have been written by a Hollywood publicist. As a rescue swimmer in the U.S. Navy, he was credited with 18 open-ocean rescues. He stopped illegal drug shipments from coming into the United States, and once saved 100 refugees on a boat that was sinking at sea. He's a bona fide hero.

After the Navy, he got a job in a call center. It was a different world, and before long he announced to his wife that the desk job was so bad he'd rather be picking up dog poop.

An idea was born.

The need is there. The rates are low. So it's no surprise that when No Doody opened in 2011, its phones started ringing.

"It was amazing," Ashley says. "People reached out to us. Before we even had the ink dry on the licensing, people were calling us. 'Thirteen dollars a week?' they'd say. 'Our kids won't even go outside for that money!'"

Are people that lazy?

"I won't say lazy," he hedges. "You maintain your yard, and when you get off work you want to go sit by the pool or sit in the yard. You don't want to smell (poop), and you darn sure don't want to step in it."

By 2017, No Doody was advertising for more employees and picking up after 200 dogs and 66 cats a week, in more than 100 yards.

Although clothes, shoes and equipment are sanitized between jobs, there's no fancy equipment involved. The "poopmobile" is a pickup truck or the trunk of Ashley's car – a harrowing tale in itself.

"When I started, it was a 2000 Nissan Sentra," he recalls. "It was horrible in the summertime of New Orleans. ... The car is baking. When the AC comes on and blows the smell through the car, it's a whole different story. You ask yourself, 'Why am I doing this?'"

Pooper-scooper businesses are established in other cities. In fact, there was a convention in New Orleans a few years back, where rowdy conventioneers played games like "who can flip it the farthest" and "toss the puck." Not your typical business confab.

But, Ashley points out, his business is more than just cleaning up an unpleasant deposit.

Dog and cat feces can contain microorganisms and parasites that are dangerous to pregnant women and people with compromised immune systems. So once again, Ashley Hauck is saving lives.

"We are more than pooper scoopers. We are an important part of society," he says. "People just don't know it yet." We've kept up with Ashley and his business continues to grow. He's moved past those eye-catching billboards and now has an equally provocative wrap that reads "GOT POOP? WE SCOOP!"

ChapterSpot

Brendan Finke and Joe McMenemon had their light-bulb moment early in college. They saw the gleam between stacks of paperwork, Excel sheets and cascades of email.

Brendan and Joe met as members of a fraternity. The off-campus frat row was the site of legendary parties and a tight-knit brotherhood. But there's more to Greek life than fun (or so I'm told). Brendan and Joe were in charge of running their fraternity, which turned out to be as much of a headache as a frat-party hangover.

"We realized that managing this organization was really difficult," Joe recalls. "We had over 1,000 different people we had to communicate with: active members, alumni, prospective members, the university, parents... plus, we had to collect over $200,000 in house dues and payments. ... It was a pretty big job for a 19- or 20-year-old."

Most fraternities were using spreadsheets and Facebook pages to organize their groups, keep track of money and manage events. It was chaotic and about as much fun as taking down a Christmas tree.

"The problem on the surface is you had all these different things you needed to do: share payments, share files, coordinate events," Joe says.

But the more basic problem was how the back-and-forth was organized. Mass emails were not going to cut it. "An active member doesn't want the same messages going to him that also are going to his mom," Joe says (understatement of the year!). "We needed to create a private social network that made it really easy for an organization to identify each member's relationship to the group. It's pretty easy on top of that to put on all these different apps: the apps to send out mass emails, send out text messages, collect payment, share files, coordinate events."

So, the duo designed ChapterSpot, a program to do just that. It was just a start.

"We know the problems of the fraternity-sorority space aren't unique to them," Joe says. "They are the same problems that Junior League has, the Girl Scouts have, that recreational sports leagues have."

Two years after launching the program with one fraternity, the duo had enlisted 1,600 chapters at 250 colleges. Some levels of the program are free, while some services, like dues collection, are available for a fee. Some National Greek-letter organizations mandated ChapterSpot as a way to organize the outreach, events and finances of hundreds of campus houses. Suddenly, the 19- and 20-year-olds managing their chapters had a ready-made structure that took a lot of the headache out of the job.

"You don't become chapter president or head of Girl Scouts or Junior League because you really like a whole bunch of paperwork," Joe says. "You do it because you really believe in the mission of that group. We're saying, look, we are going to centralize that mission and give you all the tools you need. With our power, you can focus on your mission of pushing your group forward, whatever that mission is, whatever your goals are."

If there's a chore most people hate, it represents an opportunity for someone else. All it takes is perception and the right attitude.

Peter's Principles #12

"How did I go bankrupt?

Two ways. Gradually, then suddenly."

-Ernest Hemingway

OK, so not all entrepreneurial ventures work out. Particularly the first ones. But, this book has provided you with a dozen reasons why you might want to give it a go. Remember: On their deathbeds, people often regret what they didn't do (or try) in their lifetimes. (Maybe I should have used a more upbeat rationale.)

CHAPTER 13.

Be Creative

Matt Wisdom: TurboSquid
Cathy Deano and Renee Maloney: Painting with a Twist

For a new generation of entrepreneurs, making money isn't the only goal. They've seen problems in a changing world and devised ways to solve them. Whether it's a recycling option to save the planet or a way to free up time for today's busy families, these businesses are changing things for the better.

TurboSquid

You've seen TurboSquid's work, though you probably don't realize it. And that's just fine with founder Matt Wisdom.

TurboSquid is an online marketplace for buying and selling 3D graphics: images and models that are used in everything from video games to TV commercials and movies. It serves as a platform where artists can post their work for sale, while buyers can browse and choose what they need. Think of Amazon, except for one crucial difference: TurboSquid trades in visual inventory. It's a platform where buyers shop for scary aliens for video games, tantalizing images for advertisements, and background effects for today's high-concept films.

"Did you see the movie 'Ratatouille'?" Matt asks, referring to the animated Pixar blockbuster set in Paris. "We made the Eiffel Tower."

Matt launched TurboSquid in New Orleans in 2000, and it became one of the earliest successful tech companies founded in the city. Through TurboSquid, creative people find a ready market, one where they've sold millions of images in the past two decades. Producers save untold work-hours and are able to focus on other parts of their production without having to hand-design every image in sight.

Matt is a very bright guy. But he didn't out-nerd someone in Silicon Valley (we call our growing tech scene down here Silicon Bayou — pretty cute, huh?). Instead, he used that technology to create what business schools call a platform, which facilitates interactions across a large number of participants or users. He created a place where a huge number of graphics creators and buyers could find one another.

Turbosquid (I never did find out what that name means) receives a piece of every transaction. But, without the Turbosquid platform these people would have a very difficult time finding each other.

The 3D modeling industry is relatively small, Matt says, "probably smaller than knitting. But within it, we're rock stars!" In fact, TurboSquid has become the largest online marketplace of 3D images in the world, producing models that spin, move and look amazingly realistic. The company was so successful in its niche that in 2021 Matt sold it to the New York stock photography company Shutterstock for a whopping $74 million.

Although Matt readily admits he poured 20 years of hard work into his idea, its success is something he says all of Louisiana enjoys a little bit of credit for.

The company was granted tax credits as a digital media startup, through a state program similar to the tax credits that support TV and film productions shot in Louisiana. That served as a financial cushion for the company as it developed software and created jobs in the state. "We took a lot of risk we wouldn't have taken if Louisiana wasn't supportive of companies just like ours," Matt told me.

Matt, a native of New Orleans, thinks there are solid advantages to setting up shop in a smaller town off the beaten path of big tech. Lower real estate prices mean tech companies can spend more on talent. In New Orleans, he says a culture of encouragement and support prevails, rather than cut-throat competition.

On the other hand, he is clear-eyed about New Orleans' issues when it comes to the resources that tech companies need, especially human capital. "We have had to recruit engineers from odd places, because we lack real tech expertise here," he says. "We have so little infrastructure to support our industry, no education, no capital."

While Matt's 21 years at TurboSquid were a big success, he has had plenty of ideas that never caught on with the buying public, he says. All of them taught him something, though. "You have to fail to succeed," he says, acknowledging what so many entrepreneurs have learned. "It's so painful. The thing is, you have all these great ideas, and it's not your best idea that survives." Sometimes he finds himself asking, "why this one?"

Smart and idealistic, Matt earned a history degree at Brown University and has a big-picture view of society and trends. He served on the New

Orleans mayor's transition team and is deeply invested in trying to make the world a better place.

One "great idea" that face-planted was called VoteIt, an online platform that would have allowed people to weigh in on large group decisions, for example at businesses. "I was trying to help people to decide things all together," he explained. "You could all vote and everybody's vote could change at the same time, and you're writing comments about why you support something or don't like something."

However, clients were in short supply.

"It turns out that if you are trying to democratize decision making, management won't pay for it," Matt says. "The last thing power wants to do is give up power — and pay to give up power. It was the wrong formulation for business."

From that experience, he learned that sometimes ideas are simply not right for the moment. He joked about trying to pick a superpower: "What do you want to be? More handsome or stronger or richer? I just want better timing! If you are early, people don't like your ideas." He ticked off early online sellers of toys and pet supplies that perished because people weren't ready for them. "Now," he said, "people buy all their pet food online."

TurboSquid wasn't the only New Orleans tech company that sold for big bucks in 2021. Two other homegrown startups, the research analysis company Lucid and the construction software company Levelset, were also bought for enormous sums usually only seen in Silicon Valley.

But despite his excellent payoff, Matt is still working hard. He's become what we call an angel investor, advising and investing in other promising entrepreneurs in New Orleans. He really walks the walk.

Painting with a Twist

Cathy Deano and Renee Maloney were simply looking for a way to help people feel better. It was 2007, less than two years after Hurricane Katrina, and the New Orleans area was still knee-deep in insurance claims, construction work and government red tape. What people needed, the two friends knew, was a way to relax and forget their troubles. That's how their wildly successful business, now a national chain known as Painting With a Twist, was born.

Do-it-yourself art studios have been around since at least the mid-'80s, when retail pottery studios started spreading across the country from the West Coast. Painting with a Twist takes the concept and adds something essentially New Orleanian to it: adult beverages.

People come to the studio to paint with a group of friends, have drinks and put the real world on hold for a while. A glass of wine helps painters get over "white canvas syndrome" and gets the group sharing stories and laughing.

I would think that all you need to succeed is an imagination and a designated driver. And it's probably the business professor in me but I have wondered if there was some correlation between the amount of wine consumed and the quality of what ends up on canvas.

Cathy has a story from one of their early days in their studio in Mandeville, across Lake Pontchartrain from New Orleans. "One night, the power went out," she said. "We were in the middle of the class. We told everybody, put your name on your painting, put it against the wall. We will redo the class, no charge.

"They said, 'We're not leaving.' We had big plate glass windows on the building. They got in their cars and drove around and shined their lights in the windows, and finished their paintings by the lights of the cars.

"It was a couple years after Katrina," she said. The guests made it clear: "'We don't think about the bills, we don't think about FEMA, we don't think about insurance or Katrina. We're just here to do this painting.'

"That's when we realized it was really more than painting. It was a place for people to escape."

Painters can come in for two- or three-hour sessions during the day. There are night sessions as well, and the studios can be rented for private parties. The businesses also host fund-raising events, and have donated more than $7 million for local charities by "painting with a purpose."

In the beginning, almost all the painters were women. Nowadays, Cathy says, about 20 percent are men. The studios sell out on Valentine's Day and do a brisk business on date nights. While the ladies are sipping wine, the guys, "they're the ones rolling in the full bar," Cathy laughed.

Are there other enjoyable, life-affirming projects that might go well with alcoholic beverages? Probably nothing involving fire or sharp instruments, but I'm not done working on this.

There are lots of imitators in the wine-and-art business these days. But Deano's is the largest chain. Entrepreneur's Franchise 500 has ranked Painting with a Twist No. 1 in the category — which, Cathy likes to point out, she and Renee invented — for seven years straight. More than 2,500 artists are employed across franchised locations nationwide.

Painting with a Twist wasn't a first business for Deano. She comes from a family of entrepreneurs, and has also owned a restaurant and a jewelry shop. The ideal owner of one of the painting franchises has a business background, but is also a people person. It's the kind of business that requires a lot of hands-on attention from an owner.

"The engine that drives Painting with a Twist is really about people getting together and socializing," Cathy told me. "The art is just an added bonus. It just gives them a vehicle, where they can get together and socialize, and bring home a painting from their evening. It's kind of like karaoke for art. "It is a business," she says. "But it's the most fun business you'll ever have."

Peter's Principles #13

There's a market for everything." That, of course, is ridiculous. You only need to walk through your hometown to see the remnants of businesses and products that had little hope of success from the get-go. Most of these entrepreneurs received advice from their friends, respected co-workers and family members.

These valuations are often skewed to the positive because really, who wants to tell someone their baby is ugly? It's best to factor that in.

CHAPTER 14.

Make the World a Better Place

Laurel Hess: hampr
Fran Trautmann: Glass Half Full

For a new generation of entrepreneurs, making money isn't the only goal. They've seen problems in a changing world and devised ways to solve them. Whether it's a recycling option to save the planet or a way to free up time for today's busy families, these businesses are changing things for the better.

hampr

Laurel Hess was a professional in the marketing industry in 2017 and a busy young mom when she came home from a business trip to a mountain of dirty laundry. Looming ahead was a weekend packed with tee-ball games and kids' birthday parties. There was no time to stay home and wash the clothes.

Later, sitting in the playground bleachers and ordering groceries on her phone, it hit her. Why couldn't laundry be as easy as ordering food or calling an Uber? She had a sudden realization that there had to be other busy people like her who would love nothing more than for someone to take away their dirty laundry and bring it back the next day, washed and folded.

So in 2020, Laurel launched what I like to call the Uber of laundry. It's called hampr, no E, and it's a platform to connect the laundry-overwhelmed with other people who are home with time on their hands and unused cycles in their washer-dryers.

The largest demographic of customers is busy, dual-income families with two or more kids, Laurel said. "So they're out of the home, they work a lot, and on the weekends they have kid activities ... they just don't have time. After that, it's busy bachelors."

If hampr had been around when I was younger, this service could have boosted my career. I sometimes found myself rummaging through my laundry basket looking for "the cleanest dirty shirt." You know what they say: "(Clean) clothes makes the man!"

I love this story and I'm so happy that they're expanding into other cities. I tell friends about hampr and the part that excites them is the Uber-like structure. Before I explain the logistics, most think this is about the decades-old model of a laundry pick up service bringing the clothes to a large industrial cleaning facility.

On the other side of the equation, the people who wash clothes for hampr are, for some reason, not called "hampsters." They are "washrs."

"Largely this is an untapped workforce that could not participate in the gig economy, because they had to be home for long periods of time," Laurel said of the washrs. "So it's stay-at-home parents, retirees, people taking care of loved ones at home. They haven't really been able to go and drive for Uber or shop for Shipt. They've kind of been stuck at home.

"So this is a great opportunity for them to contribute to taking care of their household, while being home and taking care of the people they need to take care of," she said.

That's what I call a win-win, and here's how it works. Customers buy a year's membership, currently $39. With that, they get four pop-up bags, each the size of a 13-gallon kitchen trash bag. They fill those up, set them outside, and notify the app. A washr claims the load, picks it up, and returns it within 24 hours, washed and folded. Customers pay a flat fee, about $10-$15 per bag, depending on the market.

"For me, it was really important that it was flat rate," Laurel noted. "A lot of laundry companies do it per pound. I have no idea how much my laundry weighs!"

Laurel is proud of hampr's personal touch. Washrs are doing this job in their own homes, using their own home appliances. Traditional commercial laundries tend to have central brick-and-mortar facilities staffed by employees — all expensive and not terribly flexible.

Word is getting around, and now washrs apply to the app. They take as much, or as little, work as they want, earning 70 percent of each load and keeping all tips.

Hampr is now available in 14 states and the District of Columbia. Two more states are joining soon. It has all the things that investors want: It's asset-light, profitable and scalable. It's done a pretty good job of raising money — nearly $7 million in the first two years.

The first institutional investor was New Orleanian Gayle Benson's Benson Capital Partners. While the female-led Benson firm saw the merits of hampr, Laurel says raising money in the South usually means talking to men. Because 70 percent of the people who do laundry are women, "we understand the pain point really well," she said, and it can be more challenging to pitch the idea to male investors.

But persistence has paid off — along with the knowledge that no matter what, families will always face those mountains of laundry.

I wonder, can innovative apps like hampr change the world? After COVID, employers — especially in the retail and service industries — were surprised to find that huge numbers of people didn't go back to work. Economists were mystified and wondered what all these people were doing to pay the rent and buy groceries.

Maybe hampr is an indicator of something going on in the wider economy. Instead of going out and getting a regular job, now people can opt to stay home — and run a laundry business out of their house.

Glass Half Full

When I was a poor college student we threw some epic parties – late nights, lots of cheap beer. The next morning we'd wake up and search the sofa cushions, but nobody had any money, and our currency would be to turn in the glass bottles, for a nickel each or so.

That doesn't happen in most places any more. Manufacturers long ago stopped buying back empties in many states. And here in New Orleans, as in many other towns, the city's curbside recycling service doesn't accept glass. While cardboard, aluminum cans and some plastics are collected, glass cannot be included in the mixed-product bins. As a result, millions of pounds of glass go to our landfills every day.

That was the situation that confronted Fran Trautmann and Max Steitz, seniors at Tulane University, in 2019. One night, over a bottle of wine, they were lamenting the fact that without any glass recycling options in town, the empty bottle was destined for the city's overburdened landfill. On the spot, these smart and socially responsible students decided to do something about that. And Glass Half Full was born.

Glass Half Full is part of a positive trend of for-profit businesses that are not only ethical and responsible, but out to make the world a better place. This company is a manufacturer of sand. Yes, sand, like at the beach! And their raw material is, you guessed it, recycled glass.

Sand is used in construction, for fill, to stuff sandbags in flood-prone area, and to bolster our recreational beaches. It's the second-most-consumed natural resource in the world, after water. And while it might seem we'd never run out, that is not exactly true.

"There actually is a global sand shortage," Fran told me. "You wouldn't think that, considering the deserts, the beaches. But the thing about deserts, that's actually a different type of sand than you can use in construction. And beach sand washes away — it has to be replenished." Dredging sand can cause other environmental problems, and we're running out of places to dredge. Meanwhile, mountains of empty glass bottles go to waste.

"Why not combine those two issues and have one solution?" Fran and Max wondered. Like many entrepreneurs, they started small. But a backyard collection station soon filled up, and Glass Half Full had to expand.

Collection points sprouted up around the city, with a positive vibe that encourages people to recycle. "That's one of our biggest goals, to make recycling this fun and exciting thing," Fran says. "Make it an event."

The atmosphere is upbeat. In New Orleans, there are always plenty of bottles to collect – in fact, the global pandemic, which cramped the style of other businesses, was probably a boon to the supply of wine and beer bottles!

"Don't be embarrassed at how many wine bottles and how many vodka bottles you have," Fran laughs. "Just embrace it! We're all in the same boat! That's how we were so successful despite being born during COVID."

The glass is sorted by color, then pulverized with hammer-mill crushers at the company's New Orleans facility. The crushed product is sifted to remove labels and other debris, then screened to produce products that range from the kind of silky powder you'd find on the beach to chunky glass gravel. Finally, the sand and crushed glass, called "cullet," is given away or sold for many purposes, from coastal restoration and disaster relief to flooring and new glass products. Some of it is remelted to become new glass bottles. The company is currently recycling more than 30,000 pounds of glass every week.

Most recently, Glass Half Full is looking at creative ways to reuse glass, such as a division called NOLA Alchemy that creates bracelets and necklaces from sparkling, repurposed glass. In the future, Glass Half Full hopes to help solve another large New Orleans problem by providing glass to make Mardi Gras beads, replacing in part some of the many tons of imported, near-disposable plastic beads that clog the streets after the yearly spring holiday.

In the long term, plans include using the recycled sand to help rebuild Louisiana's eroding coast. On the supply side, Glass Half Full has launched a home pickup service that already has a lengthy waiting list. The company aims to loop the city's bar and restaurant community as glass donors as well, tapping into a major producer of empty glass bottles.

But for now, Glass Half Full is collecting, recycling and repurposing tons of glass, creating new products from this vital resource.

"That's why glass is so beautiful," Fran says. "It can be endlessly recycled. You make a bottle, you crush it, you make a new bottle, it just keeps going and keeps going."

Since coming on our show Fran and her company have been widely featured in lots of other media outlets. These include the PBS News Hour with Judy Woodruff, the NBC Nightly News with Lester Holt and, of course, the Kelly Clarkson Show. I like to believe that her appearance on Out to Lunch was her launching pad to fame. It's not true. But, it's a funny thing to say.

One thing I've noticed, we'll always need smart, optimistic entrepreneurs like Fran and Max, who see the "glass half full." And, we'll always need sand.

Peter's Principles #14

Hiring? It's nearly impossible to get an accurate reference from one previous employer.

You never know about the relationship between the former boss and this job seeker. Furthermore, former employers are often reluctant to say anything negative because of possible repercussions. The former boss may know that this person is an ax murderer, so he says, "He was sharp!" OK, that was an extreme example.

So what is the best way to hire?

Request a few references – then **call them**. *Ask specific questions about the candidate's responsibilities, tenure and job title. Finally, ask why they left. Take your time. You should be able to piece together a decent picture if you call more than one.*

Hiring a friend or family member might seem like an easy answer, but think twice. Being someone's friend is different from being their boss, and you might lose the friendship. And if things go sideways with a family member, you could face a very awkward Thanksgiving.

CONCLUSION

Great Businesses Can
Be Built Anywhere

"Be your own lamp."

-the Buddha

Readers from other places might be surprised to learn that all of these innovative ideas are coming from people in a relatively small, sometimes struggling state. Well, that was pretty much the impetus for creating our radio show in the first place.

In 2005 Hurricanes Katrina and Rita nearly wiped South Louisiana off the map. But, a couple of years later the city had become the nation's No. 1 home for young entrepreneurs. How did they build success?

We wanted to tell that story.

In FieldsThat Aren't Sexy or Popular

To be totally honest, I don't always have a feel for which of my guests are going to succeed with their businesses. I've seen ideas with amazing potential fizzle and burn out. On the other hand, I had guests who went on to huge success when I thought their plans were off the wall and left me questioning the purity of their water supply. Timing can be everything.

And you don't want to be chasing the latest shiny thing. A business or product that's wildly popular today may not be needed next year. If people at parties are already talking about a sexy concept for a business, it's probably too late to get into it. Too late. You know, like bringing condoms to a baby shower. Definitely too late.

At Any Age

I spend most of my day with young people, and this has made me one of the most optimistic folks you'll ever meet.

I often hear my fellow Baby Boomers complain that young people are lazy, living in their parent's basements and saving up for a new tattoo. I don't find that to be at all true. I work with students at Tulane and meet smart, ambitious young guests on the show, and I honestly feel great about handing over the reins to this next generation.

They're bright, creative, community-minded and really want to make the world a better place. There will be wonderful successes, and only a fool would bet against them.

And For Very Different Reasons

Each entrepreneur has a different motivation. And there are very different ways to define success. These include building a small business, earning a good living, benefiting a community, instilling a strong work ethic in their children and eventually handing the keys over to the next generation.

At the other end of the spectrum, some entrepreneurs are unapologetically in it for the money. Their goal is to make lots of it. These folks are usually enthralled with the prospect of scaling the business, selling the business they have created and becoming very rich.

And in between, there are lots of other game plans and just as many ways to measure success.

Don't worry, there's room for everybody.

MANY, MANY THANKS.

A huge shout-out to the gang who makes the "Out To Lunch" radio show each week: our producer Grant Morris, executive producer Eric Murrell, photographer Jill LaFleur and researcher Maggie Mendel. Thanks for the laughs, camaraderie and insistence on making each show the best it can be.

And to Commander's Palace, one of the nation's most celebrated fine dining restaurants. Thanks for feeding me and my guests each week and frankly making our show "pretty darn classy."

After the pandemic our show moved to NOLA Brewing. We appreciate Doug and Jennifer Walner the affable owners of this popular spot for pizza and beer. Here, we sometimes get a bit of an audience. Because if you can't attract folks with pizza and beer, well there's something wrong.

And the law firm of Jones Walker: These folks have been underwriters of "Out To Lunch" since the show was still just an idea.

And of course WWNO, the National Public Radio station in New Orleans. Thanks for taking a chance and putting our show on the air. Much obliged.

Special thanks to Dennis Brady (architect/infielder/friend) the guy who suggested I write this book in the first place.

ABOUT THE AUTHORS

Peter Ricchiuti has taught finance at Tulane University's A.B. Freeman School of Business for 35 years. He is also the host of "Out To Lunch," a weekly business show on WWNO, the National Public Radio affiliate in New Orleans. He is a husband, father and public speaker who has attended baseball games at all 30 current major league ballparks.

Annette Naake Sisco is a writer and editor who lives in New Orleans.